Wreck, Rescue and Salvage

Captain Dick Jolly

Whittles Publishing

Published by
Whittles Publishing,
Dunbeath Mains Cottages,
Dunbeath,
Caithness KW6 6EY,
Scotland, UK
www.whittlespublishing.com

© 2006 R Jolly

ISBN 1-904445-42-X

Cover photograph courtesy of United Salvage

Typeset by Ailsa M. K. Morrison

Printed by Bell & Bain Ltd., Glasgow

Dedication

Dedicated to Roslyn, whose encouragement made this work possible, and to any old shipmates out there who may read these lines.

Contents

Chapter 1

The Call of the Sea

In March 1957, a paragraph in the local paper read:

> *Richard Jolly, youngest son of Mr and Mrs R. Jolly, High Street, commenced duty with the Merchant Navy on Tuesday. Richard, who will be a Cadet Officer, has joined the crew of the Braeside, combined passenger and cargo ship, and sails on the 29th on a four-month cruise to Singapore.*

And that is how it all began.

Having grown up in the small Victorian farming town of Charlton 160 miles from the sea, its not clear how I ended up in the Merchant Navy. My Dad was a bank manager, but an avid reader of sea yarns. I wasn't the only member of our family to be pulled towards a life at sea, however. By the time I boarded the steam train for Melbourne to join my first ship — a sixteen-year-old lad from the bush who had much to learn — my elder brother Frank had already been sailing the world on British tramp ships for a number years.

The *Braeside* was a fine modern cargo liner, built in 1949 in Glasgow and owned by Burns Philp and Company. She was on the Australia–Far Eastern run, a general cargo carrier that also had accommodation for twelve passengers.

When I joined the ship fifty years ago she was lying in Duke and Orr's dry dock in Melbourne for routine maintenance. Thinking back, she must have been one of the largest vessels to use the old wooden dry dock that was originally built for sailing ships, and now is the permanent home of the three-masted barque *Polly Woodside*. From Melbourne, the ship sailed for Sydney and Brisbane to complete loading. From Brisbane it was off to Surabaya, Djakarta, Singapore, Penang, Port Swettenham, Singapore, Rejang in Borneo and then back home to Sydney, quite a first voyage for a young cadet.

Cadets had a fairly busy schedule. At sea we were chipping, painting and polishing brass, while in port the senior cadet Alex Reid and I kept six hour cargo watches acting as tally clerks and generally assisting (or getting in the way of) the duty mate. Still, the mate was good to us lads and every evening at sea, he would have us up on the bridge for an hour before tea and try to teach us some of the ways of navigation and seamanship. He was also a source of pocket money to boost my twelve pounds a month wages.

Being a general cargo carrier, the *Braeside* was well populated with rats for which we set traps every night. The next morning the traps would be checked, and the tails of any victims cut off and carefully stored in a cigarette tin. The tin would be presented to the mate, who counted the tails. For every pair of tails, cadets would receive a bonus of sixpence.

During that first trip to sea, we spent quite some time in Singapore and I still remember the exciting runs ashore to one of the so-called fleshpots of the world.

Braeside *loading logs at Rejang, Borneo*

At that time I knew very little these things, but one night the ship's engineers took me under their collective wing and I found myself looking over a balcony in a smoke-filled Chinese gambling den. I was clutching a bottle of Lion Beer (none of the famous Tiger Beer in those days) and fully expecting to see Humphrey Bogart and Sydney Greenstreet enter the scene in their white tropical suits. However, before I could be led astray any further, the ship's purser appeared and escorted me to a picture theatre. He left me with strict instructions to proceed straight back to the ship after the show, and to report to him as soon as I returned aboard. John Lillie was the purser's name, and he took great care to see that a young country lad survived his first trip to sea in one piece.

Unfortunately, that was to be my first and last trip to sea for quite some time. While observing life aboard the *Braeside*, my young and very impressionable mind came to the conclusion that the ship's engineers seemed to have the best life of all. They did not appear to do much work and while the mates seemed to be always on duty, the engineers appeared to drink lots of beer and always be going on runs ashore. Naturally, the engineers supported this theory at every stage. They convinced me that the best thing I could possibly do was to go ashore and take up an apprenticeship at a machine shop, then go to sea as an engineer when my five years time had been served.

The memories of that first trip still come to mind. The early morning sanding and canvassing of the wooden rails around the passenger deck, the first trishaw ride in Singapore, the diminutive Chinese ladies loading huge bales of rubber in Penang: a far cry from the dusty streets of small town Charlton in the Victorian Mallee. On our arrival back in Melbourne after the adventure of a lifetime, I took my leave of the sea and of the Burns Philp Company to become a marine engineer. Everybody knew that this was the best way, and I knew better than most.

My return to Charlton was a bit of a let down, although I thrilled my former classmates from school with tales of the Far East. Those yarns took place after the Saturday night movies while drinking milkshakes in the local Greek Café, which every small country town seemed to have in those days. My former pals were either working on their dad's farm or had some very mundane job in town, and found it hard to believe that I had been so lucky. However, my Dad was disappointed with my choice of careers and to my everlasting regret, he was not alive to witness my later accomplishments. My parents were however understanding and it was agreed that I should go to Melbourne, stay with some family friends and try to pursue my new career.

In the late fifties there were a number of firms in Melbourne where a suitable apprenticeship could be obtained, such as Buchanan and Brock, Fleet Forge, Robinsons and Eblings, who were all engaged in ship repair and construction work. I was successful in getting started at the Commonwealth Engine Works in

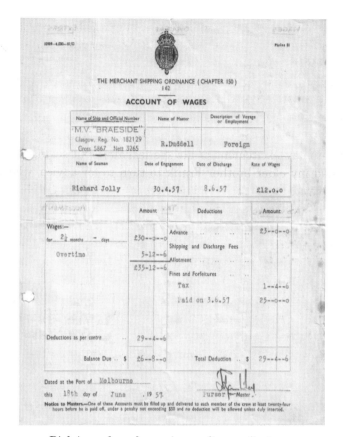

Rich in cash and experience after my first voyage

Port Melbourne, who at the time were building Doxford engines for the lake class bulk carriers under construction for the National Line. For a few months I was assigned to assist various tradesmen in the works learning the basics. I think at that stage there were nearly 600 men employed at the works, being the largest marine engine builders in Australia.

Eventually I was assigned my own lathe and I actually started to make things. At the start of the working week the leading hand would present me with a couple of large wooden crates containing perhaps two or three hundred parts. I would have to turn so much off here, drill two holes in there, smooth off this end and then pack them into another wooden box. By the time Friday evening came I was doing exactly the same thing. The highlight of our day was our forty-minute lunch break when myself and a couple of pals would race off down to Station Pier to see the ships.

Sometimes we would get lucky and manage to get aboard some of the big Passenger Liners and meet a kind engineer, who would give us a quick tour of the Engine Room. The only trouble was that this meant getting back to work late and punching the dreaded Bundy, with the subsequent deduction from our wages at the end of the week. After eight months the novelty of becoming a fitter and turner began to wear a bit thin.

While walking to the station at five o'clock on a cold dark Melbourne winter morning to take the train to Port Melbourne, with a week of repetitive work, working bell to bell for starting, smokes and knock off time ahead of me, I found myself thinking more and more about life at sea. I craved the fresh air, the sunshine, and the day-to-day excitement of always learning and seeing something new. Luckily, I had my elder brother Frank to turn to for advice, who was back in Australia and was at that time sailing second mate with the National Line. He promised to try and help me get an interview with the hope of getting back to sea.

In December 1957 I was released from the Commonwealth Engine Works and returned back to Charlton to my old job of Grocer's Boy in Mr Ellis's shop around the corner. Early in March 1958 I received my letter of appointment as cadet officer with the Australian National Line, so it was back to sea again but this time on deck as opposed to down below.

Looking at my letter of appointment the ships of the fleet are listed on the letterhead, forty-five in all, a far cry from today where the ANL has now completely disappeared and very few coastal ships remain in operation.

I went back down to Melbourne on the train again where I joined the *River Burnett*, one of a class of thirteen vessels constructed by the Commonwealth Government towards the latter part of World War II. Of about 7,500 deadweight tons, they were originally built as general cargo carriers, but by the time that I joined all were engaged in carrying bulk cargoes around the Australian coast. She was certainly a different ship to the *Braeside*, no snowy white decks or polished handrails, instead lots of rust and covered with the remains of her last cargo.

The other Apprentice was Neville Daniel who was two years my senior and one of the very few with whom I have kept in close touch right up to the present day.

I stayed on the *River Burnett* for six months carrying bulk cargoes of coal, iron ore and limestone all around the Australian coast. Unlike the *Braeside* there was not much in the way of tuition, but lots of hard work, long hours and a fair bit of playing up ashore. Our work consisted of a large amount of cleaning bilges, polishing brass work and other choice work that the mate found easier for the apprentices to carry out, rather than trying to get the seamen to do the work. My only experience on the bridge was at 0600 every morning at sea, when the wheelhouse and chartroom had to be scrubbed and all the brass polished. This included climbing up the funnel in all weathers, trying to put a shine on the large steam whistle.

In Newcastle, which was more or less our home port, we always managed to team up with apprentices from other ships, either from our own vessels or those of the BHP or AUSN Company ships. It is amazing what we used to do on our twelve pounds a month. Our favourite haunt was the *Glasgow Arms* hotel in Carrington, although it was clearly stated in my Indentures that I should not "frequent hotels, taverns or alehouses unless upon the Master's business". Both BHP and AUSN insisted that their cadets only go ashore in uniform, so their first stop would be to visit our ship and change into civvies before heading out for a night on the town.

Payday was every fortnight and when in port, I would go ashore with the second mate to collect the money from the office. Crews were on overtime then (all except the apprentices) and the money on the coast was very good. I remember feeling a bit downhearted when I lined up each payday for my six pounds and the deck boy lined up for his forty or fifty. There was always a big temptation to throw the job in and join the Seaman's Union but fortunately I remained where I was. Still, easy come, easy go. One payday Neville and myself went to the Newcastle races. I lost my fortnight's wages and gained the nickname "Perce the Punter" for the rest of my apprenticeship time.

Those first six months went by very quickly until one day in August when we sailed into Sydney. The ship was being laid up because of a lack of work and all the crew were paid off and sent home. Neville and myself booked into a boarding house in North Sydney close to Luna Park and for the next month went out to the ship by launch every day to carry out maintenance work. One day however we were summoned to the Sydney office, and Neville was sent to another ship and I was sent back to Melbourne.

By that time my Dad had retired and my parents were living in Melbourne so it was nice to get home again after a long spell away. For the next month I was kept busy working on another of the Company's laid up ships, the *River Hunter* in Melbourne. Days were also spent at the ramshackle old store that the Company had down in Flinder's Street extension. Still, all good things must come to an end and in October I flew down to Tasmania and joined the *River Loddon* in Burnie where she was discharging illmenite sand.

David Wharrington was the other apprentice, a very quiet chap and a non-drinker which did me no harm at all. In Burnie we met up with the cadets from the *Baroota* belonging to the Adelaide Steamship Company. There were certainly a large number of cadets on the Australian coast in those days and a strong bond developed between us all.

Life on the *River Loddon* went on much the same carrying bulk cargoes around the coast, however we did make two trips to Bunbury in Western Australia. This was a bonzer place for a young lad, we were always very well looked after by the locals and the longer passage back and forward across the Great Australian Bight gave us time to settle into a routine.

On that ship I spent a lot more time on the bridge with regular tricks at the wheel and gaining a few points on basic navigation. Looking back through old diaries, these river ships were certainly not fast vessels. Passages of eight knots were not uncommon especially if the ship was not loaded and in ballast condition, being rather under-powered and riding high in the water with part of the propeller exposed.

Soon my first year was completed and I flew home from Burnie in March 1959 for my two weeks annual leave.

My next ship was the *Bulwarra* one of five 'B' Class general cargo vessels. She was a motor ship of 6,000 tons deadweight mainly engaged in carrying general cargo. This was a pleasant change from bulk cargoes and a lot cleaner, plus the fact that being of a later vintage, our accommodation was much improved. During that voyage my Dad passed away and the company flew me back from Western Australia for the funeral and a few days at home.

I left the *Bulwarra* after only three months and joined her sister ship the *Baralga* in Sydney in July 1959. The *Baralga* was to be home for the next six months and a very interesting six months it proved to be. Our first port of call after leaving Sydney was Eden on the south coast of New South Wales, to load railway sleepers. Our arrival caused great excitement in the town as we were the largest vessel to berth at the port and the Sunday was spent showing hundreds of people, who had come from far and wide, over the ship. Some twenty years later I returned to Eden to live and today the arrival of a 50,000 ton woodchip vessel does not raise an eyebrow. On my return to Eden I met one of the timber workers who remembered loading the ship all those years before and we became good mates.

The railway sleepers were destined for Calcutta, so I was about to head deep sea again. Around about that time the National Line was endeavouring to secure overseas cargoes for the fleet, but unfortunately this trend did not continue, due mainly to the wages and conditions enjoyed by Australian seafarers.

We loaded 2,340 tons of railway sleepers at Eden and proceeded to Coffs Harbour to top up the sleeper cargo. Then by way of Tasmania and Fremantle we proceeded to Calcutta, anchoring off Sand Heads on September 5th 1959. On the voyage up we listened anxiously to the news, as there was rioting in Calcutta and martial law was declared the day before our arrival.

After five days at anchor the situation ashore had improved and we shifted up river to commence discharge. We spent ten days alongside with plenty of runs ashore for trips to the very pukka Calcutta swimming club (white men only) and the funeral pyres on the banks of the Hugli River. It was quite an education for a young bloke, and two things stuck in my mind: the abject poverty of the place and the beautiful 16-year-old daughter of the head stevedore. While there some of the crew went shopping for exotic wild life and this caused a lot of trouble when we arrived back in Sydney. The quarantine authorities found snakes, birds and other prohibited species all over the ship.

On the September 20th we departed down river in the hands of the Hugli pilot, a very toffee-nosed pom with his own cook, helmsman and a mountain of luggage. He was far from impressed with his quarters and was horrified to be spoken to by the lowly helmsmen or the even lowlier apprentice. From there it was a thirteen day light ship voyage to Yampi Sound in northwest Australia to load iron ore for Port Kembla. All our hours of polishing and painting soon disappeared under a thick red coating of iron ore dust. After calling into Sydney for a few days we proceeded down to Port Kembla to discharge. After discharge we commenced to load steel for Adelaide and after our long trip most of the crew went home on leave.

Lying in the outer harbour a storm warning was issued and the few remaining on board were kept hard at work tending the mooring lines as they kept breaking in the heavy surge alongside the wharf. This was before the new inner harbour was developed and Port Kembla was designated an unsafe port. At two o'clock in the morning I was woken by the mate. The wind was howling and the ship was crashing heavily alongside the wharf. Shortly after three, the moorings were slipped and we headed out to sea with all hatches open, all derricks flying and very few men aboard. We steamed up the coast and sought refuge in the shelter of Sydney Harbour. It was quite an experience and the ship made the television news that evening. If the same thing happened today, there would be all kinds of repercussions from the authorities.

After that bit of excitement it was back to work on the coast until November when we loaded another overseas cargo at Whyalla, pig iron for Japan. We berthed at the Chiba steelworks in Tokyo Bay on November 4th after a fairly rough trip and spent only two and a half days discharging. We packed a lot into that short time as Japan was still relatively cheap and even on apprentice's wages I managed to discover, amongst other things, the delights of Japanese bar girls. After discharge it was light ship back again to Yampi Sound for another load of iron ore for Port Kembla. Another year had passed and on arrival I headed home for two weeks annual leave.

Once again shipping on the coast suffered a recession and after my leave I was sent to Brisbane to join the *Binburra*, another of the 'B' class general cargo ships laid up in the Brisbane River. I lived aboard for the next six weeks, sleeping onboard and eating ashore. That was hardly the best life on a dead ship, with two lead lights and a cold shower rigged up from the wharf. Somehow, I do not think that the practice would be tolerated today. The only company I had were the enormous rats on the wharf during the night and an occasional visit from the local marine super during the day to see if I was doing any work.

Other company ships were also laid up in Brisbane so life was not too bad and at various times I was called to work aboard the *Baralga,* *Daylesford* and *Noongah.* In March I was back to sea again in the *River Burnett*, two years older and wiser than the last time I sailed in her. However, a couple of days after joining we suffered tail shaft problems and limped into Sydney to spend twelve days in Cockatoo Island dry dock undergoing repairs. This time my stay aboard was only for two months, before a couple of days at home in Melbourne before being flown across to Whyalla to pick up a brand new vessel.

The vessel was the *Mount Keira*, a 14,000 deadweight bulk carrier built at the BHP Shipyard in Whyalla. There were four apprentices aboard and the master was the dreaded Captain Ramsey. He ate apprentices for breakfast, or that is how the story went and we were about to find out. When we sailed three of us were put on watches with the fourth lad on day work.

I was on the 8 to 12 watch with the third mate, the morning watch being spent polishing brass and the night watch on lookout. Captain Ramsey did not trust the poor third mate, so he was forever creeping around the bridge checking up on us both. His verbal instructions to me were "Weather side outside, eyes all around all the time", and I never dared to go on the bridge out of uniform.

Like any new ship, we had our teething problems but after a couple of months we had settled down to regular coastal run, loading iron ore at Yampi Sound for Port Kembla. The accommodation was good, we had movies twice weekly and even a swimming pool which got a fair workout during our ten day run up north in the semi-tropical weather. Apart from the captain, life on board was fairly good. We did not have very much time in port, which resulted in an increase in study time. Combined with very good deck officers who were always willing to help us with our studies, my progress towards gaining a certificate was well on the way.

All went well until the morning of August 22nd when an incident happened that was to change the rest of my life. Passing Townsville, the stern tube began to overheat, revolutions were reduced and creeping along at four-and-a-half knots we limped in to anchor off Magnetic Island off the Port of Townsville. Shortly after anchoring, the Lloyds Surveyor came aboard but the tail shaft had completely seized. The ship had to be towed to Port Kembla to discharge her 14,000 tons of iron ore and then towed to a repair port. Head office advised that it would be another eight days before suitable tugs would be available so we settled down to wait. The only thing to happen was that I had another falling out with the Captain and was confined to the ship with no weekend shore leave. We remained at anchor but I did manage a couple of runs ashore, thanks to the mate putting in a good word for me and convincing the old man.

On Saturday September 3rd the Swedish ship *Panama* arrived off port under tow of the tug *Fearless* of Brisbane and all four apprentices watched her coming in, excited at the thought of our tow southwards. Finally the tug *Woona* (294 gross tons 1,150 ihp) and tug *Tusker* (393 gross tons 1,700 bhp) arrived on site from Sydney and Adelaide respectively. Also arrived on board was Captain John Fant of United Salvage to take charge of the towing operation.

By that time my wages were up to the princely sum of twenty pounds a month. However, the tug crews were on fourteen pounds a *day* for mobilisation and twenty pounds a day once the tow got underway. They must have been the highest paid tug crews in the world as it took me many more years to get even near that figure.

For the next few days Captain Fant, the Carpenter Len Clarke and the four apprentices worked hard on rigging the towing gear. Our crew did as little as possible as they had got it into their heads that they were entitled to 'salvage money', and many a meeting was held behind the locked mess room door, from which all non-SUA members were excluded. The Shipwright had salvage towing experience, having served on both the *Caledonian Salvor* and *Cambrian Salvor* during WW2 and was pretty knowledgeable when it came to rigging tows. However, Captain Fant took us boys under his wing and soon I was hanging on his every word. I became hooked on the world of towing and salvage, never to fully recover.

We sailed under tow of both tugs on Monday 12th September 1960. On the trip south I was on watch with the mate Mr Coates and at every spare moment I would be annoying Captain Fant for more and more information. He had brought a couple of salvage books with him which he kindly lent me, and every night I would be studying them until the late hours. They were a lot more interesting then Nicholls' Concise Guide or Thomas's Stowage, which I should have been studying.

One night on watch the captain was talking to the mate and I just happened to overhear, "Mr Mate that Captain Fant is a strange fellow, he even talks to the apprentices". What an ignorant old bastard was our Captain.

The first part of the voyage was not too bad weather wise, but as we went further south gale warnings were issued and conditions worsened. Off Sydney we were punching a Southerly gale and making no headway at all, the two tugs rolling and pitching violently and at times they could not be seen through the rain and driving spray. It was decided to go into Sydney to check the tow gear before proceeding down to Port Kembla for discharge. The boys on the tugs must have been very relieved when we finally headed in. After a short spell in Sydney, we towed down to Port Kembla to discharge, then back to Sydney to await dry docking. The tugs had done a good job, the *Woona* (Captain Powell) was basically only a harbour tug, whilst the *Tusker* (Captain Abbott) although possibly the most powerful tug on the coast, was not really designed for outside towing.

Neither vessel was equipped with a towing winch, and the *Woona* was using a combination of wire and old Manilla towline, with which I was to become well accustomed some years later. Our good Captain was well out of his depth during the towage operation and even with my limited knowledge, I well understood why Captain Fant had been placed aboard to see that everything went off smoothly.

Captain Fant must have put in a good word for us with John Williams (later Sir John) who was Chairman of the National Line and also Captain Fant's boss at United Salvage, for we all received a nice letter and what's more a week's leave with air fares paid. While at home I typed out a towing report, the first of many, and informed my mother and sister that I had found my calling in life. No more cargo ships for me, tugs and salvage as soon as I had finished my time. One day I went into the city and spent a fortnight's wages on two books: *Lloyd's Calendar* and *Marine Salvage Operations*. I was committed to the way I hoped to shape my future career.

Back in Sydney we all stood by the vessel during repairs, carried out in the Naval dry dock at Garden Island. The only other dock capable of handling the *Mount Keira* was located in Brisbane, which would have meant another long and expensive tow. While there a tragedy occurred to the Naval stores carrier HMAS *Woomera*, which blew up and sunk off the Heads with the loss of two lives.

Tugs Tusker *and* Woona *towing* Mount Keira

After completing repairs, I remained on the *Mount Keira* for another five months. Luckily for me Captain Winter also joined during this time and life aboard was much more pleasant for all. Life went on as normal, except for when heading for Yampi Sound once and a cyclone had severely damaged the place before our arrival. We were then diverted to Whyalla to load our ore cargo, which meant a complete circumnavigation of Australia in a single voyage.

In February 1961, the *Runic* ran aground on Middleton Reef. I heard that the tugs *Woona* and *Fearless* attended, and thought of my friend Captain Fant. I wished that I had been there with him on the attempted salvage.

In March I went back home for two weeks annual leave before flying to Brisbane to rejoin the *Baralga*. Captain Ramsey had rejoined the *Mount Keira* so I was glad not to return there, however Captain Howard (Paddy the Pig) proved to be my next challenge. The *Baralga* was on the Western Australia run carrying mainly steel products. We visited a large number of ports and as I was then into my fourth year, the cargo handling and maintenance of the cargo gear was all good experience.

Shortly after joining *Baralga* another tragedy occurred off the Queensland Coast, the *Verao* (ex-ANL's *Ransdorp*) sunk 190 miles off Brisbane with loss of life. Meanwhile salvage attempts on the *Runic* had been abandoned, she was stripped and her bones left to rot on Middleton Reef.

The next five months spent on the *Baralga* went fairly quickly, a lot of ports, too much playing around and trying to make up for lost time with the studying. On one occasion we loaded a full cargo of barley at Port Lincoln for Melbourne. It was a slow process taking a fortnight to load 5,000 tons using the ship's gear and loading from a number of small ketches, the names of which have long been forgotten. When the *Baralga* was headed off on another overseas voyage, I was transferred to the *Lake Illawarra* to give one of the other apprentices the chance of getting away from the coastal trade, as I'd had two overseas trips with the company previously.

The *Lake Illawarra* was a 10,000 on bulk carrier, later to claim notoriety in the Tasman Bridge disaster of 1975. I joined her at Newcastle in August 1961 and was mainly employed in the Whyalla iron ore trade but was only aboard for a little over two months. Looking back through my diary, I seem to have not been real happy aboard the *Lake Illawarra* and was very anxious to finish my time. A series of run-ins with the master while desperately trying to keep on the straight and narrow and to learn as much as I could before going ashore for my ticket made life none too pleasant.

I well remember one night leaving Newcastle. To say that the captain and the mates had enjoyed a very social stay in port was an understatement. I had been on duty from early morning, helping the stevedore to load (no sign of the mates).

At about ten that night I was on the bridge testing the gear prior to sailing and remained there assisting our captain to see his way out of port. Somehow we made it out safely and the Old Man staggered down below and left me to it. There was no sign of the third mate so I kept watch until midnight. I tried in vain to wake the second mate for his watch and when he refused to get out of his bunk, kept the 12 to 4 watch as well.

At four in the morning both the AB on watch and myself tried to call the mate, again without result, so by now feeling very weary I remained on watch. Finally at eight that morning, both the third mate and our captain appeared on the bridge. Immediately our captain started to quiz me on the Rules of the Road. I refused to answer and was told that I was useless and would never obtain my ticket. Such was life on the Aussie Coast (in the days before drink driving).

In October I was paid off and sent to Melbourne to attend a Radar Observer's course and then it was off to Sydney to finish my time aboard the *Binburra*, the vessel that I had been assigned to earlier when she was laid up in Brisbane. A week after joining, another of the company's ships *Wangara*, went ashore just inside Port Phillip Heads and I listened to all the radio news broadcasts to see how the salvage attempt was getting on. It took United Salvage about five days to refloat her, but she was severely damaged and was still in dry dock when I left the ship some six weeks later.

I was back with my old pal Keith Sharp as the other apprentice and Neville Daniel as third mate. Keith and I were both going up for our tickets at the same time so we did a fair bit of study but also did a fair bit of boozing to celebrate our last trip. Six weeks after joining it was all over and on December 28th I flew home to Melbourne. My four years as an apprentice had finished and I was not sorry, now it was up to me to get stuck into the work, get a second mate's ticket and start my career in salvage.

Chapter 2

From Apprentice to First Mate

At the start of 1962 I enrolled in the Nautical School at the RMIT in Melbourne. Also in the class for second mate were Keith Sharp and Mike Hodgeman, two of my fellow apprentices from the National Line. Captain Pearson was in charge of the school and for the next three months it was head down and bum up, to try and make up for all the time wasted in the last four years. That's not to say we didn't lead a fairly active social life at the same time, but money was scarce and none of us really enjoyed the confines of the classroom after four years at sea.

On March 26th I submitted an application for examination which was duly accepted. I then borrowed some money from my mother and purchased a new suit for the occasion. Then on one day in April, three very nervous lads presented themselves to the Examiner of Masters and Mates in the old Rialto Building in Collins Street.

The examinations took a full week. I refused to take part in the discussions regarding answers with my pals after we left the examination room, but just hoped for the best. The three of us all passed our oral examination, but when the results of the written examinations were issued, unfortunately for the other two, I was the only successful candidate.

The day I was handed my 'blue slip' was a cause for much celebration, as the rule was that you were meant to show that magic piece of paper to every barmaid in town. However, it was all very well to have a brand new certificate in my pocket, but I was stony broke and it was time to get back to work. My career in towing and salvage would have to wait until finances improved, so I went knocking on the door of the National Line once again.

At the end of May I joined the *Timbarra* as third mate lying at Newcastle loading coal for Melbourne. The *Timbarra* was a 10,000 ton bulk carrier built in 1954, but she was of a very old design with a triple expansion steam engine and the two ships of that class did not remain very long on the coast.

Nor did I remain very long in the *Timbarra*, for after just two and a half weeks we steamed into Sydney and the ship was laid up. The next job was not long in coming however, and I joined the *Boonaroo* as third mate in Melbourne. The *Boonaroo* was a sister ship to the *Baralga* and *Bulwarra* on which I had served my time, so at least I knew my way around. Captain Ellis was the master and he was a great encouragement to a young third mate who was very much learning the ropes. During the two months that I was on board, we loaded general for Darwin and then around to Yampi Sound and loaded iron ore for Newcastle.

Overtime was still going strong in those days and as third mate my average earnings were about fifty pounds a week, quite a change from twenty-four pounds a month as a final year apprentice. When we arrived back in Sydney in August, I had a few hundred pounds in my bank account and a great desire to see the world, so my days of coastal sailing were over. Quite a number of the lads with whom I had served my time remained on the coast, reached the rank of master and retired. By that time, however, I had had enough. The ever-present industrial strife both on ship and ashore, the monotony of the bulk cargo routes, plus the fact that if I was ever to achieve my ambition to become involved in salvage, meant that the sooner I got myself to the UK the better.

On arrival in Sydney in August 1962, I contacted the local Bank Line Office as they were always on the lookout for people and within four days I joined the *Roybank* as second mate in Wallaroo in South Australia. The *Roybank* was an Empire Class ship built in Sunderland in 1945 of 7,368 gross tons, with British officers and Indian crew. My pay as second mate was sixty pounds a month plus six shillings an hour overtime, quite a big change from the coast. That difference in wages was the main reason why so many remained with the National Line for their full sea careers.

After delivering a load of phosphate to Adelaide we sailed for Christmas Island in the Indian Ocean to load another phosphate cargo, that time for Albany. So there I was back on the coast, carrying bulk cargoes and getting paid about 25% of what I could be earning. Things were not looking good: the food was pretty awful, the beer was warm (no refrigerator aboard) and the master was a grumpy old bastard.

Fortunately for me on the other side of Australia on another ship, the chief engineer got drunk and smashed a bottle over the head of the second mate, one ended up in gaol and the other in hospital. After discharging at Albany we proceeded to Fremantle where I was immediately paid off and was sent across to Townsville to join the *Firbank* as second mate. The poor bloke I relieved in hospital was none too happy, but I was delighted.

So after only six weeks aboard the *Roybank* I joined the *Firbank* which turned out to be my ticket to the UK She was a more modern ship of 6,318 gross tons and had been built in 1957 at the same yard in Sunderland that my previous ship had started her days. Townsville was her last port and she was discharging general cargo before heading up to the islands to load cargo and then back to the UK. Once again she carried British officers and Indian crew and they all turned out to be a really good crowd to sail with. Even the master, Captain "Deep Tank" Moody, was a very pleasant but rather eccentric character, with whom I got along very well. I was soon to learn where he got his nickname from.

From Townsville we did the rounds of the islands, loading copra, cocoa and coffee. First stop was Gizo in the Solomon Islands, then Samarai, Rabaul, Kavieng, Rabaul and Madang. The sacks of copra were lifted aboard using the ship's gear and then spilt and poured down the hatches. Loading was slow and took nearly a month at the various ports.

We worked very long hours but I did not mind, as we managed to get some good runs ashore and the old man did all his own pilotage with myself on the bridge to assist him. It was different and interesting and I was sorry when we were finally fully loaded and on our way to Colombo for a crew change.

The deep tanks were loaded with coconut oil and there I saw the old man in full form. He was very particular with the cleanliness of the tanks as the coconut oil was a very valuable cargo. After the crew had cleaned the tanks, he had them filled with water again and then jumped in wearing his jocks and armed with a scrubbing brush. As the tanks were pumped down he swum around with his little scrubbing brush to make doubly sure they were clean, hence the name 'Deep Tank'.

One afternoon on watch while crossing the Indian Ocean, I observed a line of warships approaching. Signalling them with the aldis lamp, I learnt that they were in fact six new 'Ton' class minesweepers for the RAN on their delivery voyage from the UK.

As second mate, part of my duties was medical officer and every morning I would open up the dispensary to a long line of Indian crew that were always waiting. Being new to the game I fell prey to their tricks. They would come clutching their head, their stomach, their big toe, whatever. "Oh Sahib, plenty pain, please Sahib give me tablet". I gave them tablets but they never seemed to get any better as they were always back the next day. Only later did I learn that if they went home with enough pills, they could set themselves up as unofficial medicine men in the village and make some money. Anyway, good luck to them, as they worked hard for very little pay and did a full two years aboard the ship before going home on leave.

Our reason for visiting Colombo was that the crew were due for leave. We arrived and made fast to a mooring out in the stream on November 27th with the crew due to go ashore that evening. The mate told me that the barge was due alongside to take the crew ashore and to get the derricks ready. I thought that he was pulling my leg until a tug with a bloody great barge in tow came alongside.

Then the crew went ashore; I was amazed. Every man had at least four or five suitcases, several wooden crates and empty oil drums ingeniously altered to carry stores, countless sewing machines and bicycles. Very soon the deck of the barge was covered — the ship must have risen a good six inches out of the water when all their dunnage was finally discharged. More amazingly, when the new crew came aboard, they were the most schooner-rigged crowd that you could have imagined, but I daresay two years on it would be a different story.

The next day we sailed from Colombo and then it was across to Aden for bunkers, a short stay there and up the Red Sea to the Suez Canal. My first trip through the Canal was an eye-opener, unfortunately there were many more transits in years to come and none of them ever became any better.

A few days before Christmas we arrived in Liverpool to discharge. There were some problems in getting the company to release me, as they wanted me to sign on for another voyage. However, articles were closed, and after I had signed an agreement that I did not require to be repatriated to Australia, there were no further objections to me signing off. The mate then asked me about my plans and as they were non-existent, he invited me to spend Christmas with his family in Wallsend-on-Tyne. I thought that the Indian crew had some gear, but the Mate had been aboard for two years and he was loaded.

Amid a great pile of suitcases, sea-bags and cardboard boxes (plus a half-wild cocky in a cage) we boarded the train at Liverpool station one evening bound for Tyneside. The weather was extremely cold and as we had already drunk our docking bottle, Barry (the mate) went in search for something to keep us warm and returned with a carton of miniature whisky bottles. It was quite a memorable trip and we finally arrived at Newcastle station early the following morning.

In the taxi Barry made a confession, he had not telephoned his wife that morning, in fact he had not written home for months. Full of booze and camaraderie he told me that if he hammered on the front door, I should run round to the back and catch the lodger. Fortunately, there was no lodger but his wife was none too happy to be woken up at three in the morning by a couple of drunken sailors banging on the door, accompanied by a squawking cockatoo.

By the next morning everything had settled down. He produced boxes of presents and souvenirs, his wife was happy and the young Aussie he had brought home fascinated his three teenage daughters. That was the first of many visits to the household; in fact it became my second home for a number of years. People were amazed when I would say I was going to Newcastle for my holidays, but the people in the shipyard and mining village of Wallsend were amongst the nicest and friendliest folk that I ever met and May and the girls treated me as family.

The local pub was the *Engine Inn*. The place was full of coal miners and on a cold winter's night, their whippet dogs would surround the fire in the bar. Once I had mastered the Geordie accent and the locals understood my strine', I was always made most welcome. Between the Working Man's Club, the whippet races, the flat beer and the three daughters, I always had a hard time pulling myself away from the place and going back to sea.

However, after a couple of weeks I took the train to London and started knocking on doors. I went around all the towing companies that had offices in London but ended up very disappointed, nobody wanted to know a young Aussie with no towing experience and a brand new second mate's ticket. My new career was getting off to a bad start.

Money was beginning to run short, so I joined the MNAOA which was the Officer's Union in those days. They procured a third mate's job for me on a ship called the *Norse Coral*, a new 14,000 ton general cargo ship operated by R. Nerdrum Limited that was loading in London for the United States. My wages were fifty-eight pounds a month plus a ten pound hatch bonus for the trip in lieu of overtime.

The following morning I arrived at the company office in Crutched Friars and was driven down to Dagenham in no less than a chauffeur-driven Rolls Royce (two months after I was fighting for my wages). She was loading cars from the Ford plant for the United States and was fitted with portable car decks especially for this trade. We sailed on January 25th 1963 with some 1,400 cars bound for Newark, New Jersey. The voyage across was rough with continuous gales and snow squalls. As third mate, I would spend about three to four hours every afternoon armed with a torch doing the rounds of the car decks checking and tightening up the lashings. When I joined the ship she was half-loaded and unknown to me she had loaded cars on special platforms in the deep tanks, so those went unchecked.

On a bitterly cold day (12° Fahrenheit) we anchored off New York on January 27th. I went down to the midship gangway to meet the Port Officials, where despite us having a very large Red Ensign flying from our stern, I was greeted with a call of "Hey, do any of you guys speak English?" We carried British Officers and Chinese crew, our port of registry being Nassau in the Bahamas. Because of our Chinese crew, we had an armed guard aboard to see that nobody jumped ship and to put it bluntly the guards were a pain in the backside, treating all of us as though we were illegal immigrants. We discharged at four ports and loaded at a fifth (Newark,

Baltimore, Savannah, Jacksonville, Norfolk) and the ship was arrested five times for non-payment of various bills. No writ nailed to the mast in this modern age, but a notice sellotaped to the steering wheel.

After discharging our cars, including some very bent and broken ones from the deep tanks, we prepared to load a full cargo of 14,000 tons of grain for home. This meant dismantling the car decks and rigging shifting boards for the grain. The master and the second mate, who was quite elderly, kept continuous anchor watches. The mate and myself split the deck crew into two gangs and worked a good 14 hours a day down in the holds. That was where the ten pound 'hatch bonus' came in — and we earned every penny. There was no shore labour to assist and the mate (Mike Poskitt) kept asking me why I had ever left the Australian coast? I must admit sometimes I wondered myself.

As mentioned the second mate was an elderly bloke and a bit grumpy, but here my luck changed. When I told him that my wish was to get into the towing and salvage game, he informed me that he had spent most of his life doing just that, and gave me a contact name and address back in England. I immediately wrote a very polite letter to the Admiralty and sent it off *poste haste*.

We sailed on February 22nd arriving back in London on March 5th after a very rough Atlantic crossing and commenced discharging. Following on from our

Norse Coral *Atlantic Passage*

problems in the States, we had some problems getting paid at the close of articles. The owners (Nerdrums) had gotten into financial difficulty and the vessel was subsequently taken over by Silver Line and was re-named *Totem Star*. I stood by for another week for the new owners as they had invited me to stay on, but on arrival the letter I had posted from the States had been answered and I declined their offer.

After a couple of days in London I took the train down to Bath and had a meeting with Mr Edward Singer of the Admiralty. He was in charge of the crewing of the Royal Fleet Auxiliary vessels including their towage and salvage division. Our meeting went very well, he could see that I was very keen to get started and promised to do his best to get me into the service. However, he did explain that a lot of formalities and checking up had to be done before a new recruit could be accepted.

So it was with high hopes that I returned to Wallsend and was given a good welcome home. On April 2nd, I received a letter from Mr Singer saying that the formalities were still proceeding, but inviting me to join a tug in Portsmouth the following week, initially as a guest. I immediately telephoned him to accept his kind invitation.

I arrived in Portsmouth on April 8th 1963, left my gear at the station and

RFA Typhoon, *my first tug (courtesy of Wright and Logan, Portsmouth)*

armed with my letter of appointment entered the gates of the Navy dockyard. My new ship was the RFA *Typhoon* and she was the biggest tug that I had ever seen. Built in 1960 she was 200 feet in length and over 1,000 gross tons. She looked squat and powerful, but dwarfed by the aircraft carrier that was lying just ahead of her.

She had a large crew, 32 all told with most living in Portsmouth. They had been together a long time; the whole crew had been transferred from the steam tug *Saucy* (a wartime built 'Assurance' Class rescue tug) when the *Typhoon* was commissioned. She carried a master and two mates and I was signed on a supernumerary second mate.

The Master was Captain Jones, a real down-to-earth gentleman, and I am pleased to say that we got on very well from the day I joined. The mate (Des Hazell) was a very serious fellow and I always thought that Des should have been in the Navy proper, however we became good friends and he was a good shipmate. The second mate was a real old piss-pot but it is thanks to him that I ended up on *Typhoon*, the flagship of the salvage fleet. The remainder of the crew ranged from young to ancient, and were a good mob of blokes and my time spent aboard *Typhoon* was very enjoyable. Thinking back, I was extremely lucky to get such a start as it was very doubtful that I could have gained a job on commercial deep-sea tugs with my limited experience.

The day after I joined, the Mate came to me before lunch. He was on his way home for the day and told me that the only job for the crew that afternoon was to load the beer and then they could finish up and have the rest of the day off. A couple of trucks came alongside and we loaded 100 five gallon kegs which were stowed down the ship's magazine. This set me thinking: it must be thirsty work, this towing caper?

On April 10th we sailed for Malta. The Bay of Biscay lived up to its name and for the first time ever I was seasick. She was an excellent sea boat but a lot smaller than anything I had been on before. Thankfully the seasickness did not last and has not troubled me since.

On the passage south I kept the old man's watch, after the first watch he could see that I knew what I was doing and he left me to my own devices. During that first trip I was billeted in the ship's hospital. That was a bit rough but I was happy and after eight days at sea we entered Grand Harbour, Valetta. We had two small tows to pick up, an Admiralty motor fishing vessel and the water tanker *Spaburn*. As was usual with the RFA, the dockyard rigged both tows, but we still managed to spend about nine days in port before getting underway for Gibralter.

The MFV was dropped off at Gibralter and after a couple of days there, we continued on to Pembroke to deliver the *Spaburn*. That was the only double tow I was involved with in the RFA, towing one off the towing winch and one off the hook.

After delivery we returned to Portsmouth and tied up to our usual berth for two weeks before our next assignment. It was certainly a hard life in deep-sea tugs. On arrival back at Portsmouth my appointment was confirmed and I was promoted to full time second mate. The old man was happy to see the other second mate go as he was unreliable. It was quite warm in the Mediterranean and he used to go on watch at noon with a carafe of iced water. One day Captain Jones told me to sneak up and have a sip out of it. I did this and so help me it was almost pure gin. Captain Jones did not have the heart to sack him although he knew what was going on, so he was transferred to another tug that spent even less time at sea than we did.

Our next assignment was a bit of a disaster, we spent a week towing a 350 ton *Dracone* around the English Channel on trials. The concept was good for transporting fuel, but unfortunately the design was not the best as it kept falling to pieces and breaking the towing connection, so no more trials were ever forthcoming.

For the next six months we did a fair amount of towing around the British coast: minesweepers, destroyers, landing craft, tugs, barges, submarines and even a double tow with the tug *Bustler* with a floating dry dock. Every tow was different and it was all good experience.

Between tows we spent quite a bit of time in port and there were lots of good runs ashore. Portsmouth was a really good sailor's town, and the 'Aussie from the tug' became well known in various waterside pubs. I distinctly remember falling madly in love with the barmaid from the *Shipwright's Arms*.

In August 1963 we changed Articles and all hands had a fortnights leave. I took the ferry from Liverpool to Dublin and spent the time wandering around south Ireland. There were not too many tourists over there then especially in the out of the way places and I had a great time. Everybody I met had some distant relation in Australia and to say that I was made most welcome, is certainly an understatement.

One evening I had arrived in a small village and hearing sounds of merriment coming from the grocer's shop, I wandered in. The grocer's turned into the local after-hours bar with a group of very large Irishmen sitting at the bar drinking Guiness. Not to be outdone I ordered myself a beer, silence descended and you could hear a pin drop. After a short time, the largest of the group approached me and demanded to know, in a rather threatening manner, which part of England I came from. When informed that I was born and bred in Australia, the frown immediately dropped from his face. Several hours later, after consuming numerous pints of Guiness and many choruses of 'Wild Colonial Boy' and 'We're Bound for South Australia', I staggered out, promising to return to spend another night with all my new found mates.

After one of the most enjoyable holidays I can remember, it was back to the *Typhoon* and straight down to Gibraltar. For the next three months we were shuffling minesweepers from Malta to Aden towing through the Suez Canal. On the first transit, the mate Des locked himself in the chart room with the echo sounder recording the depth and, peering out the porthole, making copious notes of military installations. Hence my theory that he should have been 007 instead of tugboat mate.

We returned to Portsmouth one night in late November. The dockyard linesmen were full of rumours, we were sailing the next day for Singapore to tow home nothing less than the aircraft carrier *Ark Royal*. The old man was handed instructions to take on full fuel, water, stores and to be ready to sail at short notice. There was great excitement on board and I thought that this would really be something to write home about.

The following day was a busy one. We loaded the ship with full fuel and fresh water tanks, took on three months supply of foodstuffs and topped up our beer and bonded stores. As navigation officer, I started digging out folios of charts, sailing directions, tide tables and other publications to make sure that we could find our way there and back. There was still no official word of our destination, but sailing time had been posted for the following morning. That night I went ashore with two of the lads to toast our departure. We were a legend in our own minds and fairly swaggered up the road, as opposed to staggering back home quite a few hours later.

The following morning we sailed still not knowing where we were bound. Standing on the bridge with the old man, he went to his cabin, opened the safe and returned a few moments later with our sealed orders.

"Proceed to Gibraltar at best speed for further orders."

This was it, I could visualise it already, the crowds and the brass bands on the wharf as we proudly towed the *Ark Royal* into Portsmouth. The *Typhoon* worked her way up to her 14 knots full speed and sailed south towards Gibraltar. On arrival we berthed alongside and waited for orders. After a couple of days they came:

"Return to Portsmouth."

So home we went again and we never heard any more about our trip to Singapore or the aircraft carrier.

After a few more coastal tows it was time to go on leave. I paid off a few days before Christmas and headed back to Newcastle. Just prior to going on leave Captain Jones called me into his cabin and showed me a letter asking for a volunteer to join the fleet tug in Singapore as second mate. He told me what a good billet this would be and strongly advised me to put in for the position. So it was that I left *Typhoon* with some 17,000 miles of towage experience under my belt and great deal of confidence for the future.

I took his advice and was accepted for the job. However, I had arranged to take special leave to attend school and study for my first mate's ticket prior to flying out to Singapore. I commenced my studies at the Warsash Nautical College in Southhampton at the beginning of the school year of 1964. I remained there for only six weeks, before successfully obtaining a First Mate Foreign Going Certificate. I was not over impressed with Warsash; it was run like a toffee-nosed public boarding school. Cadets marching up and down outside the gates with wooden guns, cocktails before pig swill in the dining hall and generally quite out of touch with reality.

Fortunately there were a few like-minded individuals in the mate's class. We found some good local pubs and generally had a good time, as well as putting in the long study hours that were required. Most of those attending the college were from the big liner companies and there was definitely some sort of class barrier between those gentlemen and myself, a lowly Tuggie and a colonial at that.

In the first week of April, I boarded a services charter flight to Singapore to join my new tug at the Sambewang Naval Base. She was the steam tug RFA *Encore* of 780 gross tons and 1,800 ihp. She was built as a rescue tug in 1944, 175 feet in length and had been fitted with a towing winch.

She carried British officers and Chinese crew, a total of about 30 if I remember correctly. The other relief officers and myself joined her early one morning and were greeted by our predecessors clutching bottles of whisky and all fairly well tanked. This was not a good sign as we had joined on a two-year contract and I wondered if I would be in the same condition when my contract came to an end.

She was certainly different for a deep-sea rescue tug, not the vessel itself but some of the attachments. The bridge and forecastle had snowy white canvas awnings rigged, forward under the awning were cane chairs, tables and potted palms. On each wing of the bridge was a large domestic refrigerator, one for cold cuts, one for beer. As mentioned she was a steam tug built for the North Atlantic, so had no air conditioning, one boiler always flashed up and a coal fired galley range. Lying alongside the Naval base in the heat of Singapore, it was like living in an oven, no wonder the fore deck was so well fitted out with all home comforts.

We all soon settled into the routine and it was a good thing that our pay was supplemented by various bonuses. I was paid the board of trade rates for second mate, plus 10% extra for having a first mate's ticket, plus 10% hard lying allowance for tugs, plus 35% Far East station allowance.

Every morning in port we would all assemble on the forecastle, then at ten o'clock (not a minute before) the buzzer would be pressed and a white-coated steward would appear. The order would be placed for six cans of Tiger and we would have our first beer of the day. At noon we would go up the road to the Officer's Mess, HMS *Terror*, for a few beers before lunch and then a few beers

RFA Encore *in dock at Singapore Navy Base*

after lunch. Three o'clock and back to the tug for a couple of hours sleep, up again at five, a quick shower and then head ashore for a night's drinking. Sometimes we went into Singapore itself, usually the nightclub on the roof of the Seven Stories Hotel, or across the causeway into Johore Bharu, or maybe just to one of the bars in Sambewang village. It was a hard life and I reckoned that I would probably be dead well before my two-year contract was completed.

Very occasionally we went to sea. This consisted mainly of day trips target towing off the east coast of Malaysia, or perhaps going to sea with PTAs (Pilot-less Target Aircraft) which would be fired off our after deck and worked by radio control to 'buzz' various units of the fleet. It was quite interesting work, but in the four months I remained in the *Encore* we spent a grand total of ten days at sea. On one of those rare trips we managed to run aground off Changi. The vessel was holed and taking water, so the mate and myself went to break out a couple of salvage pumps only to discover that all the suction hoses had been sent ashore for overhaul and had not been returned. However, we managed to get back alongside the salvage depot at Loyang and get some pumps aboard before going into dry dock the following day.

Apart from rapidly ruining my liver, pickling my insides and destroying brain cells, I was not accumulating any sea time for my master's certificate. Luckily, I found a friend in the Base Salvage Officer, who like myself was a civilian and understood my problem. One morning he called down aboard and drove me into Singapore. There, we boarded a launch and went out to the tug *Salvonia*, which was lying on salvage station in the Eastern Anchorage.

The *Salvonia* was owned by Overseas Towage and Salvage Company of London, one of the companies to whom I had unsuccessfully applied for a job some time before. She certainly looked a bit more business-like than the *Encore* and talking with the mate on board, she was kept very busy on towage and salvage work. The captain said that their second mate was due to go on leave and he would be willing to employ me in about one month's time.

I immediately sent in my resignation to Bath quoting the lack of sea-time as being my main concern. This was duly accepted and a week later I was packing my gear and trying to unload an accumulation of paraphernalia that I had gathered for my two year stint in Singapore, including but not limited to a motor bike and a bloody great stereo system. As I had not been home for quite a while, I told the master of *Salvonia* that I would fly home and get myself back to Singapore when I received a cable to do so. He was happy with this arrangement and I was anxious to get home after almost two years, so ended my career with the Royal Fleet Auxiliary. But at least I was on the way to realising my ambition of joining commercial deep-sea tugs.

As it turned out I never did join the *Salvonia*, which was possibly a very good thing. The day of my visit was in July 1964 which was the only occasion that I saw the ship, for some four months later she was lost in the South China Sea when trying to salvage the Panamanian ship *Pompadour* aground on the Bombay Reef, seventy miles from Palawan.

Chapter 3

The World of Commercial Tugs

It was nice to get back to Melbourne and catch up with the family and meet a few old shipmates after two years away. However after a month at home I had still heard nothing about my appointment to *Salvonia* and sent a telegram to the London Office of Overseas Towage and Salvage Company.

The reply was not good. They declined the use of my services, being under the false impression that I would demand repatriation back to Australia. To say that I was angry was an understatement; I was furious as I knew that after tendering my resignation to the Royal Fleet Auxiliary there was no way to become reinstated. There was only one thing to do and that was to go to London and bang on their door and demand a job. Money was a bit short, so instead of flying over I booked passage on the *Fairstar* and sailed from Melbourne on August 26th 1964.

The *Fairstar* was new on the coast; that was only her second voyage on the UK–Australia run. From Melbourne we sailed to Sydney, Brisbane, Singapore, Colombo, Aden, Suez, Naples and Southampton, arriving there on September 29th. It was a good trip despite sharing a four-berth cabin down in the bowels of the ship. I fell in with a crowd of young Aussies whose main purpose in life was to party. This we did from sailing right up until we berthed in Southampton. On arrival in Singapore, nobody was allowed ashore because of riots, but luckily I had a yarn to the purser and he arranged for the agent to pick up my baggage from Connel House Seaman's Club where I had left it six weeks before.

The trip through the Suez Canal was most enjoyable, propped in the air-conditioned bar and watching the crew putting up with all the hassle. I shook the hand of the master-at-arms, after he had put the deck hose on some of the Western Oriental gentlemen who were causing trouble on deck, wishing that I could have done the same thing on previous occasions.

On arrival in the UK, I bunked in with three of the lads who had got themselves a flat in Earl's Court (where else). The next day they were all out looking for work, while I just lazed about for the next two weeks and took in the sights. In due time I presented myself at 24 St Mary's Axe, the head office of Overseas Towage and Salvage Company. My arrival caused some consternation, but the manager, Mr Wintersun, was very apologetic and promised me a position in the company immediately.

Returning to the flat that evening my pals were quite amazed that on my first day of looking for work, I had a job at sixty seven pounds a month when they were working for an average weekly wage of six pounds. I shouted them out for a night of celebration and promised to keep in touch, which of course we never did.

I joined the *Britonia* as second mate, lying off the Isle of Wight on the 26th October 1964. She was only tiny compared to *Typhoon*, but was newly completed only the year before. She was 568 gross tons, 157 feet in length and powered by a 2,000 hp British polar main engine giving a maximum speed of 14 knots. *Britonia* was to be my home for many months to come and life was certainly very different from in the Royal Fleet Auxiliary. Firstly our crew only numbered fourteen in total, we rigged all our own tows and very rarely did we get harbour tug assistance.

Our first tow was the boom defence ship *Barbastel* from Plymouth to Cobh for scrapping. Cobh in Southern Ireland was one of our regular salvage stations when between jobs. Other salvage stations in the UK were Falmouth and Dover, although at those ports there was usually too much opposition. During the winter months in Falmouth you would usually find a tug from United Towing (British) plus a tug from Smits (Dutch), and at Dover there would always be a Bugsier (German) tug on station. A far cry from today, when the British Government pays out good money to have ETVs (Emergency Towing Vessels) on station around the coast of the British Isles; back then the job was done with no cost to the taxpayer.

After a short spell at Cobh we towed a small drill rig off the Dutch Coast, then across the Atlantic to the Bahamas. There we picked up the small reefer ship *Maha* for towage to Genoa in Italy. The ship had loaded a full cargo of grapefruit and had lost main engine power plus refrigeration, so all the way across the Atlantic we left a trail of rotten grapefruit that had to be dumped overboard.

Our new Captain who had joined us in Cobh was causing concern, he had been sprung by the agent in Genoa while paralytic drunk and I am sure that a full report had been sent back to London. From Genoa it was down to Aden to pick up the bucket dredger *Hercules* for towage to Rotterdam. On our early morning arrival at Aden our captain went ashore with the agent and myself and Willy Wilson, the mate, spent the day rigging the tow and securing the vessel for sea passage. All hands had worked hard through a stinking hot day and everything was now ready for sea, so at about five o'clock, we broke out a cold case of beer and all sat relaxing on the after deck.

No sooner had the top been ripped off the first can when our gallant captain arrived back aboard with the pilot. He yelled abuse saying we were a mob of useless drunks, staggered to the bridge and collapsed on the deck a gibbering mess. The bosun went forward to heave the anchor, Willy went aft to stream the tow and I went to the bridge with the British pilot.

The pilot shook his head with disgust and stayed aboard an extra hour after we had cleared harbour, until the tow was streamed and I was happy to take control. He was a nice bloke that pilot, he shook my hand on leaving and said he was glad that it was me and not himself who had to sail with the Old Man, who was snoring peacefully on the deck of the wheelhouse.

During the transit of the Suez Canal we had a repeat performance and the sooner we arrived in Rotterdam the better. However every thing went well for the remainder of the voyage until we reached the Western Approaches to the English Channel.

A distress call was received from the Spanish coaster *Morcuera* (700 gross tons, built 1961). She was on fire and about to be abandoned by her crew. We steered for her position making our best speed of six knots with the dredger towing astern. Fortunately the weather was good and on arrival the work boat was dropped and myself, the cook and one seaman went aboard.

The fire had almost totally destroyed the accommodation block and was still burning fiercely. I reported by radio back to the tug and asked for a tow wire and three inch pump to be sent over in the hope of saving her. This was duly delivered and hauled aboard, the boat returned to the tug and then to my dismay, tug and tow disappeared over the horizon: the Old Man was into the sauce bottle again.

Myself and the cook remained aboard the casualty, rigged up a towline forward and managed to douse the worst of the flames with the portable salvage pump as there was nothing much left to burn. Taking the corner off number three hatch (closest to the fire), I managed to crawl over the cargo and feel the after bulkhead. It was cool to the touch, so hopefully the cargo would not ignite through heat transference. I also passed up a box of the tween-deck cargo to the cook waiting on deck to see what we were carrying. The box contained cut glass decanters of premium whisky, so as it was mid-winter and very cold we went right forward and sampled a bottle. So it was on a dark winter's night in the middle of the English Channel, we huddled in the lee of the forecastle hoping to see the tug return, sipping on a bottle of Scotch. Within an hour the tug appeared alongside and we were illuminated with a powerful searchlight.

Unfortunately it was not our tug, but the German *Hermes* and I asked the cook could he swim? The Germans listened to our story and remained standing by, which was a comfort as we were completely alone. A couple of hours later and *Britonia* appeared once again, the towing connection was made and myself and the cook gladly returned to the warmth and shelter of the tug.

Twenty-four hours later, the dredger was handed over to the Smit tug *Clyde* and we proceeded to Dover with our prize. All went well and tug and tow arrived safely, we were all pleased to arrive and what was even better, standing on the wharf with our general manager was Captain George Leggate, our new skipper. Our old skipper disappeared into the sunset never to be seen again, and I for one was not sorry. Captain Leggate turned out to be one of the nicest and most competent masters with whom I ever sailed. I am pleased to say that I kept in touch with him until his passing in 2000. He was an excellent teacher and highly respected by every member of the various crews who sailed under him.

During the next month after leaving Dover we carried out a series of coastal tows around the UK and near continent before proceeding to Rotterdam (Maassluis) to change Articles and undergo a minor refit. All hands were paid off and we went on leave back to the UK, Wally Martin (chief engineer) and myself standing by for the first two weeks of the refit.

Maassluis brings back many memories as I fell madly in love with a barmaid from the local café and our relationship lasted for over two years. However as this is a tale of the sea, I think that I will take the liberty of omitting further details. Needless to say I enjoyed Rotterdam very much, and before we sailed again I managed to return to England for two weeks and visit the folks in Newcastle.

By this time the company was still run from London, but the Dutch firm of L. Smit & Co. Internationale Sleepdienst had come to some sort of financial arrangement and were having more say in the day-to-day running of the three tugs under the Overseas Towage and Salvage banner. As a result, our home port became Maassluis, the small harbour off the New Waterway which had been the headquarters of the Smit Tugs for many years and now houses the Dutch Tug Museum.

During that refit, the tug was brought up to Smit's standard, in that a relatively large amount of salvage equipment was placed aboard that we did not previously carry. Extra pumps, ground tackle, fire fighting equipment, patching material and diving gear were loaded into the salvage hold.

We left Maassluis early in April and after towing a floating crane from Leith to Amsterdam, sailed down to Ostend to tow the tug *Ocean Bull* to Palermo in Sicily. We then travelled around to Taranto, the famous Italian Naval Base to pick up a double tow for the Red Sea. We did not know what to expect as we were told that the smaller of the two tows had a width of over 160 feet. What we found was a barge loaded with drilling equipment, and an offshore drilling platform on its side, floating on two narrow pontoons. This was in the early days of offshore construction and today such a structure would not warrant a second look, but at the time it was quite novel to us.

Once again the weather was kind across the Med, which was a good thing as the pontoons dipped completely under water in any sea, placing great strain on the holding down bolts and clamps that secured the actual platform to the pontoons. Our passage through the Suez Canal presented the usual hassles and I was very glad that Captain Leggate was now with us and not our previous skipper. Canal tugs were employed to assist and I remember one of the Egyptian tug skippers coming aboard to borrow some bulldog grips, in order that he could make up a towing line.

One day into the Red Sea and both tows were passed to the Smit tug *Tyne* (386 gross tons, built 1944). This was to happen on a regular basis, however in handing over the tows, we also handed over an amount of new towing and salvage gear aboard the tows and received a heap of junk in exchange from the Dutchman.

After transferring our tows it was off to the Persian Gulf to stand by the crane barge *McDermott 9*, which was engaged in offshore construction work. This was definitely a job that we were not cut out to do, as *Britonia* was too large and awkward to handle in the close confines of oilfield construction. However, we remained there for six weeks in the stifling heat without any air conditioning. Occasionally we would be fast alongside the barge overnight and could go aboard and sit in air-conditioned comfort to watch a movie. All good things must come to an end and we finally departed from the Persian Gulf on July 13th. We were soon to be back there again however, this time with another salvage job.

The southwest monsoon was at its height when we poked our nose out of the Gulf of Oman and into the Arabian Sea with a heavy sea and swell running and strong winds. Late in the afternoon we received a message relayed from the tanker *Alnair*, saying that they had sighted a broken tanker at position 18°37' north, 57°48' east and was going to investigate. We immediately altered course towards the given position and kept in radio contact with the *Alnair*. Some two hours later she informed us that all the crew had been safely rescued and that she was proceeding towards the Gulf. She also stated that the after part of the casualty was low in the water, while the fore part was capsized and at times completely disappearing from sight.

The tanker was the *Hejaz*, 14,000 deadweight tons, built in 1954. She was fully loaded and had broken in half just forward of the bridge amidships. We came across the after section later that night and stood by with our searchlight illuminating the wreck and warning passing ships to keep well clear. The following morning everything was prepared and somehow in the atrocious weather conditions, managed to get the work boat away with Chief Mate Willy Wilson and four crew, together with towing pennants, shackles and portable radio. The work boat was secured alongside the casualty using the ship's heavy mooring ropes and the boarding party scrambled aboard the heaving wreck.

Willy soon had the heavy towing pennant rigged at the tanker's stern and George Leggate eased the tug into position for connection. Standing on the towing deck at times waist deep in water I thought that we were going to end up on the wreck. Despite the thirty-foot swell and howling wind George took us close to the casualty and held us there whilst the connection was made. Our skipper earned our utmost respect that day. The *Britonia* was single screw with direct drive, meaning only a limited number of engine movements before starting air ran out, and not the easiest thing to handle on a calm day let alone in those prevailing conditions.

Finally the tow was fast and we slowly steamed away downwind, streaming fathom after fathom of tow wire until 1,500 feet separated tug and tow. Then it was time to get the boys back to the safety of the tug. The motor boat was rapidly being smashed to pieces against the side of the casualty, and at times thrown completely clear of the water. The boys made their leap aboard and were just about to cast off when disaster struck, the propeller became fouled with a loose rope, there was no way of clearing it and once again they jumped back to the deck of the tanker. The motor boat broke adrift soon after and sailed away, never to be seen again.

Now our only option was to try to tow in towards the coast, get into some shelter and try to get the men off. We were only about 20 miles from Ras Madraka where shelter could be obtained. The course was set and at about one-and-a-half knots tug and tow made their way north.

We found a shallow open bay and anchored at four in the morning. Both anchors were down and steaming slow ahead, the wind continued to howl but we were sheltered from the sea and swell and relatively safe. For the next four days we hung in waiting for the weather to ease. Our days and nights on the tug were bad enough, but for the boarding crew on the casualty the situation was becoming desperate.

Very early in the morning of the 5th day the casualty was winched in to about 200 metres. A rocket line was fired across the gap, followed by a heavy messenger rope with which we floated down an inflated life raft attached by another messenger line to the tug's winch. The raft was pulled back alongside the casualty; the boarding crew scrambled aboard and were slowly heaved back to the tug. Soon five weak and bedraggled figures were helped aboard. It had been a close thing but now all hands were safe and well, I do not know who was the most relieved, the boarding crew or us.

Within the hour, the tug's anchors were raised and once again we headed north towards the Persian Gulf, dragging our unwilling charge behind. The weather improved as we steamed further north and speed was increased to three-and-a-half knots. The Smit tug *Thames* (664 gross tons, built 1961) turned up to assist and on August 4th, the casualty was safely moored off the port of Bahrein using two salvage anchors from our tug. She still had an estimated 8000 tons of gas oil remaining aboard and we all looked forward to receiving a good bonus at the end of the trip. Given the age of the tanker and the cost of fitting a new bow, she would most certainly go for scrap, but there had to be some salved value remaining, goodness knows we had earned it.

I must add that after my episode with the *Morcuera* and her cargo of whisky, once the tow was connected, Willy Wilson did a thorough search for the bonded stores locker. Only to sadly realise that having the name Jeddah as her port of registry, the *Hejaz* was strictly an alcohol-free zone.

Our next tow was another floating crane from the Red Sea to Trieste and another transit of the Suez Canal. In Suez, George Leggate went on leave and Captain Alf Sims joined. We delivered the *Micoperi 12* safely to Trieste and then rendezvous'd with the Smit tug *Schelde* (423 gross tons, built 1958) off Sardinia where we took over the tow of the small passenger ship *Bremerhaven* for onward towage back to Trieste.

The night we anchored off the *Schelde* in Palmas Bay, we noticed much activity and unloading of pumps from our tow, however nothing was said by the Captain of the *Schelde*. Before getting underway, Alf Sims placed two men aboard with portable pumps for the run to Trieste. Subsequently, it was discovered she was leaking badly and the boys were pumping for about eight hours a day, or else she would never have arrived at her destination. From Trieste it was to Arzew to pick up one of Risdon Beazley's salvage vessels, the *Topmast 18* which had been working in Algeria, and to tow her home to Southampton.

Due to the construction of a vessel, a maximum speed limitation was incorporated in the towage contract which was a sensible precaution. In my opinion, this speed clause is not adopted widely enough, especially if an inexperienced tug crew is involved, who often mistakenly think the faster you go, the quicker you arrive at your destination.

It was certainly nice to get back to the UK again and after delivering our tow, we docked in the King George V Dock in Southampton. The poor little *Britonia* looked lost in that giant dry dock. I stood by for a week and then proceeded on a well-earned leave.

I had been aboard for thirteen months and clocked up another 20,000 towing miles. My month's leave was soon over, split between Newcastle and the continent, and in no time I was on the plane to my least favourite destination: the Suez Canal. Originally I had been earmarked to go out to our tug *Marinia* (396 gross tons, built 1955) which was station/harbour tug in Bermuda, but unfortunately plans were changed and I was sent back to *Britonia* as first mate. I joined her in Port Said (Alf Sims master) where she was passing through on her way south with a bucket dredger and hopper barge in tow for Bushire in the Persian Gulf. The weather was a lot kinder than last time in that region and we had a fairly uneventful passage, but I hoped that we would not be stuck in the Gulf for so long that time.

From Bushire it was across to Kuwait where we spent two weeks alongside waiting to tow two barges out to Singapore. At least we were alongside and every evening we would wander up to the Souk, drink tiny cups of very strong coffee and listen to the local music. Our bonded store was sealed on arrival — the temperance society would have been proud of us. The weather was hot and I was as dry as a Pommie's towel just hanging out for that first cold beer.

Finally we sailed with our two barges in tow for Singapore, the *London II* and *London IV* loaded with construction equipment. At this stage Vietnam was hotting up and any construction plant that would float was heading towards the Far East. Upon our arrival at Singapore, Alf Sims went on leave and Captain Leggate rejoined. We took on bunkers and the next day continued on to Da Nang with our two construction barges. That was to be first of many visits to that Vietnamese port. Sailing from Da Nang we proceeded light ship to Hong Kong. That was my first trip to Hong Kong, and I remember trying to drop the anchor with a very persistent Chinaman climbing all over me with a tape measure. He won, and two days later I strolled ashore very smart in my new tailor-made tropical suit.

A very pleasant eight days followed with lots of good runs ashore, pretty girls, cold beer and not much work being done. Once again I was pleased to see my friend George Leggate back on board, for we were now ordered to South Korea to take a triple tow to Vietnam, and I knew that George's vast knowledge would come in handy for that one. We arrived at Inchon on March 1st and anchored off in the stream. Our tows were three US Army barges, each 130 feet long, brought out to us and lashed up alongside.

Like myself, George believed in 'one tow — one towline'. Towing in tandem one behind the other put all the eggs in one basket, with no control of the overall length. If the towing gear happened to part, there was little chance of recovery. So we connected chain bridles, fore-runner pennants and nylon stretchers to each barge. Two barges connected to our double-barrelled towing winch and the third on a long tow wire turned up on the cruciform towing bollard. All the gear was rigged and the nylon stretchers were flaked on our after deck and connected. By knock off time everybody was just about stuffed, so after a couple of beers it was early to bed with just the watchman on duty. However, we had visitors during the night and one of the 30-fathom double nylons was eased over the side and cut both ends. That turned out to be a rather expensive night, as towing gear is never insured. Anyway, we soon replaced our stolen rope and proceeded down the river in thick fog.

The three tows were streamed successfully with no collisions and we made seven knots for the 2,000 mile passage to Qui Nhon in Vietnam. On arrival in Vietnam nobody wanted to know us. We anchored in the bay, secured all three tows alongside and recovered our towing gear. Finally some American major came aboard and asked what we were up to. When George quizzed him about the barges the reply was, "Well Captain, we sure don't want the damn things here, so I guess that you best take 'em back to where you found them".

Poor old George was furious and stated that in two hours time he would cut them loose and sail away. This brought results and soon our three charges were taken away and we were heading for Sasebo, Japan. At Sasebo I was relieved and flew back to Europe on a very rough old charter plane via Anchorage, Alaska. Beside three men from *Britonia*, there were four Dutch tug crews aboard the flight. The booze flowed non-stop during the long flight but with the crew also getting into the party mood, it was quite a relief to touch down in Schiphol Airport.

I had secured a job in our tug *Marinia*, but not working for Overseas Towage and Salvage. She had been purchased by Salvage Engineers, Hong Kong (currently Semco Salvage) and the offer of three times the rate of pay I had been receiving was too hard to pass up together with the promise of quick promotion. At the beginning of April 1966 I boarded the *Marinia* which was tied up in the old berth at Maassluis. Captain Ron Ross was the skipper, and we were old friends as Ron had been chief mate with me on the RFA *Encore* in Singapore. We did a lot of work on the old girl to get her ready for her long steam to Singapore and picked up a scratch crew for the delivery voyage, most of whom Ron had dragged out of various pubs in the UK.

The chief engineer, Fred Buzza, was an old salvage man having worked on *Ocean Salvor* belonging to Ship and Cargo Salvage of London, but none of the others had ever set foot on a tug before. Still, early in May we sailed for Singapore and arrived some five weeks later. The voyage was uneventful although we sat with our ears glued to the radio hoping that somebody would get into trouble and present us with a salvage job, but no such luck.

On our arrival the run crew was paid off and a Hong Kong crew joined. The five officers decided to stay on and after a few months, you could not have wished for a better crowd to sail with, all quickly became converted tug men. From Singapore we sailed to Saigon, where the company had quite an extensive dredging programme going on. However, our job was to run a shuttle service with barges across the South China Sea between the Philippines and Vietnam, working directly for an American construction consortium. Ron Ross left on arrival at Saigon to fly back to the UK to pick up an old tank landing craft that the company had purchased. The idea was to sail her out to Singapore and then convert her to a shallow draft salvage vessel. As it turned out she did finally arrive, was converted, and that one ship was responsible for the ultimate success of the company.

I went off to see the British Consul (the ship was still registered in London) and obtained a permit to sail as master on my first mate's certificate, a practice that I don't think would be allowed today. However, I soon had the piece of paper in my hand, everything was legal and I was about to embark on my first command. From Saigon we towed an empty barge to Poro Point in the Philippines, which became our base. Then it would be two loaded barges to either Da Nang or Qui Nhon and two empty barges back to Poro. We were carrying mainly prefabricated bridge and wharf sections which were manufactured in the Philippines for construction in Vietnam.

The *Salvana* (as she was now called) was not an easy tug to work, she had no towing winch and all tows were off the hook, or more correctly one off the hook and one off the towing cruciform. After a while our Chinese crew proved themselves to be big ship sailors, who were definitely not suited for deep-sea tug work. After consultation with the Singapore office, Filipinos replaced the crew. They mainly came from Luzon Stevedoring Company (a local towage and salvage firm) and were well able to handle the work.

Our after deck was not all that big and with the two sets of deep-sea towing gear flaked on deck ready to stream, there was not too much room left. Our barges varied in size from 120 to 270 feet in length and one had to judge the correct length of tow before starting, because once you were out at sea, nothing could be done to alter the lengths.

We struck some pretty foul weather across that stretch of water including days of overcast conditions with no sights to determine position and the occasional typhoon thrown in for good measure. Our worst trip from Poro Point to Da Nang towing two loaded barges was done at an average speed of two-and-a-bit knots. We struck the tail end of a typhoon and limped in with the lower accommodation flooded and a smashed lifeboat, but both barges were delivered safely. Even though they were both half flooded, no deck cargo had been lost.

Poro Point was a good town, off limits to the American Forces at nearby Clark Air Base, so we had it all to ourselves. We soon had the *Tugman's Inn* established, a local bar decked out with life rings and a large red ensign pinned up on the wall. Right next door was the local rest house where the boys could relax after hours.

However that same red ensign caused us no end of trouble one night when a crowd of American seamen came in off one of the cargo ships in port. They objected strongly and wanted to punch out any Limeys present. Fortunately, a quick telephone call from the Mama San and my little mate, the district chief of police turned up with jeep loads of troops and the Yanks were marched back to their ship at gunpoint and told not to return.

Vietnam was a mad house, nothing was organised and everybody was on the make. One trip we got stuck over the Vietnam side for longer than usual, fresh stores were impossible to obtain so in desperation I went aboard a Yankee stores ship to try and buy some fresh vegetables. The captain was very good, but pointed out that a staggering 40% of the stores went missing before they were safely secured in a warehouse ashore. After a while I made other arrangements and we never went short again.

One time in Da Nang we were tied up at a newly built wharf some miles from town waiting for our barges for the return tow to Poro Point. Over a few beers we decided it would be a good idea to go uptown for the night, but how to get there? The chief engineer wandered ashore to fix our transport and returned about an hour later driving a US army truck that he had 'found'. We piled aboard and set off driving through the jungle towards town. After a few miles we came across a roadblock (luckily one of ours). The Yanks pulled us up, telling us it was too dangerous to continue our journey. They promptly laid on two armoured jeeps and drove us into town, saying we could pick up 'our' truck up in the morning. We accepted the lift but did not bother returning for the truck. I could easily quote a long list of similar incidents where such confusion reigned.

Some months later a new skipper arrived with a proper ticket. He was another big ship man but after quite a few near disasters, the chief engineer and myself decided that it was time to move on. I resigned from the company and flew to Singapore to pack up the flat and then head back to England. It was time to go to school again for a higher certificate, and that time I enrolled at the Nautical School in Hull. I was aiming for a Tugmaster Foreign Going Certificate and as Hull was the home of United Towing Company, I thought that the school would have had a lot of experience in teaching that particular course. It was a really good school, a bit run down but with none of the bullshit associated with Warsash. As soon as one of the instructors, Captain Armitage, heard I was up for tugmaster, he took me under his wing. It was the first certificate of its kind that they had dealt with for years and Captain Armitage was an old tugmaster who had written a textbook on the subject.

I lived in the Merchant Navy Hotel, which was a bit of a trap leading to a rather hectic social life. Each Friday night after school, one or more of the instructors would come in for a beer and a yarn; it was just that type of place. Six weeks later I fronted the examiner and in March 1967 was granted Tugmaster Foreign Going Certificate Number 22.

I was offered a job with United Towing as Navigator on the *Welshman* that was about to depart to West Africa with a tow. Going aboard I was given a very cool reception and when I asked the Master about towing gear, I was told that it was none of my damn business, my job was to navigate and nothing else. So I told him he could do his own bloody navigation, and back to the Merchant Navy Hotel I went. United Towing had a system going. The masters were without deep-sea qualifications and a navigator would be employed with a deep-sea ticket to keep things legal. If anything went wrong, the bloke with the ticket would take the blame but at the same time had no say as to the running of the tug or the conduct of the towing operation.

Anyway, it was too cold to hang around the UK so back to Singapore I went. Here like so many before (and after) me, I was conned. An individual who shall remain nameless, ran a few small coasters and I was offered a position that was going to lead to greater things. The wreck that I was supposed to sail on never even left Singapore, and I am still waiting for some of my pay. After a while I woke up, cut my losses and headed back home to Melbourne after an absence of nearly three years.

It was nice to be home again and I did a bit of relieving work as mate on the tugs in the Melbourne River and a trip offshore to stand by an oilrig. But in Australia there was no salvage work or deep-sea towing going on and I decided to write to my old firm Overseas Towage to see if they had anything to offer.

In August 1967, I flew to Durban in South Africa and joined my old ship *Britonia* as first mate. Captain George Crawford was skipper and most of the crowd were old friends; it was just like coming home again. We lay at Durban on salvage station for over two months with no results. Twice we sailed to render assistance: the *Atheni* ashore a constructive total loss, and the *Kent* broken down in the Mozambique Channel, but no assistance was required. Life was good in Durban, we lay alongside not too far from town and enjoyed the South African hospitality. The only bad point was that all this idle time was rather hard on the hip pocket, once again being back on Board of Trade wages.

Our first job was to tow the large jack-up rig *Ile de France* 2,000 miles along the West African coast, this we did with Smit's tug *Clyde* towing in tandem. As mate I watched with envy every morning as the Dutch crew washed down the tug with fresh water. The *Clyde* was fitted with a water maker whereas we were not, and fresh water was hoarded on a long voyage.

After delivering our tow it was light ship across to Antigua in the West Indies. On our arrival, there were quite a few of the crew up to see the doctor (away from home too long), some replacements were flown out, but we ended up sailing short-handed. From Antigua we picked up two barges for Marseilles. The weather was kind and the 4,000-mile tow was completed at just over six knots. We dropped our tows off the port and it was back to Rotterdam to close Articles and pay off.

On arrival at Rotterdam, I received word that Mum was terminally ill and the company very kindly flew me straight home to Melbourne. Mum passed away within a few days of arriving home and I was glad that I had made the effort to visit just a few months before. After sorting out a few loose ends, there was nothing to keep me in Australia.

To rejoin OTS would mean getting myself back to England, so it was back to Singapore. I joined Selco Singapore as master of the salvage ship *Salvista*, the old wartime landing craft that had been converted for salvage and mooring work. Of 400 gross tons and 190 feet in length, she was fitted with bow lifting horns with a nominated 200 ton lift, powerful winches and two sets of heavy ground tackle.

A few small lifting jobs and work on single buoy moorings occupied a couple of months, and then we assisted in the salvage of the tanker *Blythe Adventurer*. The ship had run aground off Horsburgh Shoal in the Singapore Strait, fully loaded with Naptha spirit and ripped 18 of her 36 cargo tanks open. First job after refloating was to run her aground in a selected location. Standing on the bridge guiding her ashore was quite an experience. Cargo was discharged over the top to a series of small coastal tankers, using air-driven submersible pumps as hydraulic tanker transfer pumps had yet to be invented. The whole operation was fraught with danger and the risk of fire and explosion was ever-present, especially working with equipment that was never designed for the job. During the operation, I had a falling-out with management over safety issues and when the job was finished went off to seek pastures new.

My old mate Fred Buzza was in town and here I must relate a very amusing incident. He was visiting Singapore for a few days and invited me to go with him to Ipoh in central Malaysia where he was living. About eleven one night, we boarded the train at Singapore and settled into the first class lounge car. The jungle rolled past as the train chugged its way up the Malay Peninsula. Fred and myself were arguing about what kind of engine we had; he said a 4-6-2, I said a 4-8-4 or something along these lines. Anyway we decided to get out at the next stop to count the wheels of the steam engine and see who was correct. When the train pulled up at a small jungle clearing we alighted and walked up to inspect the engine.

The Indian fireman was delighted to see us and proudly invited us up to inspect the cab. This we were happily doing when the driver returned, a nasty Aussie. "What are you bastards doing in my engine, get off!" We jumped to the ground and the driver hit the throttle and the train rapidly started to move.

"Jump for a door!" yelled Fred. We both jumped, my door was locked, but luckily Fred's was open. As the train sped through the dark jungle I hung on for grim life, until after what seemed like forever Fred found a porter to unlock the door. We never did find out how many wheels the engine had.

Chapter 4
Dutchmen and Dead Ships

In August the tug *Neptunia* (500 gross tons, built 1949) arrived in Singapore for a crew change and I signed on as first mate. My old mate George Leggate was skipper and for the next twelve months, the *Neptunia* was to take me all over the world. Our first job was the rescue tow of the Norwegian cargo ship *Hoi Ying* that had been badly damaged in collision in the South China Sea. Next we relieved the Smit tug *Witte Zee* towing the oilrig *J W Nickle* in the Karimata Strait, while she went to Singapore for bunkers and a crew change. The *Witte Zee* was 9,000 ihp and had been towing the rig at six knots, but although we were only 2,000 ihp we still managed to tow it at four!

We relieved another Smit tug, the *Loire* (384 gross tons, built 1952) of her tow off Minicoy in the Indian Ocean and delivered it to Singapore. Then it was back to Hong Kong to pick up double tow of a floating crane and a barge for towage to Singapore. No sooner had we dropped our tows off in Singapore than we were heading at full speed back to the South China Sea. The wartime built *Agenor* (ex-*Fort Michipicoten*) was abandoned in a sinking condition off the south coast of Vietnam.

We found the casualty on November 3rd with a US coastguard cutter standing by with her crew on board. Weather was fairly good so George managed to put the tug alongside whilst I scrambled aboard for an inspection, what a bloody mess. I had seen better ships in the scrap yard. She was in ballast, had a seven degree list and was well down by the stern. On closer inspection the engine room, stokehold and numbers four and five holds were flooded to sea level and the bulkhead of number three hold was starting to bulge under pressure. George asked my opinion and we decided to give it a go. Pumps and towing gear were passed aboard and two men and myself went along for the ride.

When they saw what was happening the master and chief engineer of the casualty also returned aboard. However, the rest of the crew refused and the entire Greek crew transferred across to the tug from the USCG vessel, which promptly shot through and left the whole disaster in the capable hands of the tug. The tow was rigged and we got underway towards Singapore. Two diesel salvage pumps were rigged in tandem in number four lower hold, however little progress was being made with de-watering. We stopped pumping as darkness fell, lit the oil navigation lamps and crashed out on the bridge wing using life jackets for pillows, just in case she decided to take that long plunge during the night.

The following morning we managed to close the shaft tunnel door and pumping of the after holds started to show some results. Then we tackled the worst job of all to empty the ship's freezer of rotten foodstuffs before we reached port. We carried no breathing apparatus, so it was down below, grab an armful, up on deck and toss it overboard, then throw up.

As we pumped the list slowly came of the casualty and we made a steady five-and-a-half knots, arriving at Singapore anchorage on November 6th. Once anchored, the sea intakes were plugged externally, the ship pumped out and returned to her owners. It was then we sighted the master and chief engineer who had remained in the skipper's cabin, drowning their sorrows for the entire tow and not offering any assistance in trying to save their vessel.

Then it was back again to Hong Kong, this time for two hopper barges bound for the Persian Gulf. That time we only made it to the Bay of Bengal, where we met our old friend the *Loire* and handed over both tows. We returned to Singapore and the *Loire* went to the Persian Gulf. I definitely think that we had a win that time. A few days before Christmas it was down to the Karimata Strait to rescue the fire-damaged American survey ship *United Geo 1* and return him safely to Singapore. On Christmas Eve we received what we considered a rather strange order from London, to sail for New Plymouth, New Zealand to tow a bucket dredger to Whangarei. In other words steam 5,000 miles to carry out a 500 mile tow?

The run down from Singapore was very pleasant, and when George learned that I had sailed through the Barrier Reef on previous occasions we took the inner route much to the consternation of the London Office, who were convinced that we were ashore when they received our noon position reports. On January 14th we arrived at New Plymouth. I was at my station on the after deck so I did not witness the exchange between the pilot and our skipper, but apparently it went something like this...

Pilot: "You have come a long way to do this tow, Captain. "

George: "Yes Pilot, I cannot understand coming all this way to tow only 500 miles. "

Pilot: "500 miles, Captain? I thought it was more than 500 miles from here to Rotterdam."

We finished making fast and the bosun and myself were just about to open a can of beer, when a very agitated George came banging on the cabin door.

"Dick come in to my cabin now!" so in I went. I was told to sit down, presented with a paper and told to sign it. He wouldn't tell me what it was, so I just signed. "Congratulations Captain," said George, "I'm going home".

So that is how I took command of the *Neptunia*. George did the right thing and stayed on for the first leg of the voyage around to Whangarei where the dredger was slipped prior to the long tow home. George left us in Whangarei and a new mate was flown out from the UK. 105 days and 13,103 miles after leaving New Plymouth we arrived in Rotterdam with tow intact, all crew still sane and a rather proud master.

When I say all crew sane, I do not know if I should include the runners. Three Dutchmen joined us in New Zealand to ride the tow home. This was their full time job, riding dead ships at the end of a towline from one end of the world to the other. These blokes were a special breed as I am sure that I could never have done their job. Stuck on a dead ship, a coal fired galley, a couple of hurricane lamps, no refrigeration for fresh food and absolutely nothing to fill the time. Their only break was daily radio contact with the tug, and if the weather was good, maybe once a week we would drop the boat and send them back some fresh stores or if the cook was in a good mood, he would maybe cook them a roast dinner.

First stop was Papeete for bunkers. Managed to get two days in for some relaxation and then next stop Panama Canal. Four days out from the canal, I sighted a passenger ship on the horizon who called me up on the radio. He asked where we were bound and how long we had been at sea, and then asked if we had any women aboard. When I replied that the only female was the ship's dog, he said he had 500 beautiful young Australian girls aboard and he would get them all out on deck to wave to us. The next thing he had altered course and passed us very close alongside at slow speed. He must have made an announcement over the public address system for the decks were crowded with all his passengers waving and cheering; it was quite a sight to remember.

Weather was good and the 4600 miles were covered at just under six knots. After leaving the canal, the weather worsened and the dredger started making water, the runners earned their keep and with continuous pumping we made it into Kingston, Jamaica where the problem was rectified.

Two days after sailing from Kingston, the runners called up from the dredger. They had just discovered a stowaway. The cunning bugger hid himself for two days knowing that it was too far for us to turn back. Despite a telegram from London telling me to land him on a desert island, we took him on board the tug off the Azores, as the poor bloke was getting a bit of a hard time from the Dutchmen and he was nearly blue with cold.

We towed into the New Waterway on May 3rd, harbour tugs relieved us of the *Noord* and the tug berthed alongside in Maassluis. Our guest was escorted ashore by two burly Dutch police and I daresay he was back in Jamaica within a few days. The following day I was invited to Smit's head office, taken to lunch with one of the Directors and told that I had done a good job.

When I took over in New Zealand the company sent me out a Memoranda for Masters Guidance. This consisted of eight typewritten pages covering just about any situation that I might encounter. Today, in a world driven by paperwork, rules and regulations, this would more likely fill eight volumes.

Three weeks later it was back to Maassluis and then three tows around the UK coast, including a dredger from Dublin to Rotterdam and another from Rotterdam to Milford Haven. Unfortunately, there was a brand new crew and apart from one engineer and the radio operator, none of them had had any previous towing experience and this made the job bloody hard. After dropping our last tow in the Bristol Channel, we were ordered to Amsterdam to pick up a floating crane. This turned out to be the semi-submersible *Choctaw* — at that time the largest floating crane in the world. It was not until we arrived in Amsterdam that I was informed that she was heading for Bass Strait, Australia.

I remember arguing with the Yank owners for a daylight sailing as we had to tow down the *Noord* Sea Canal and through the locks at Ijmuiden before entering the North Sea, definitely a daylight job. The Yanks wanted to save twelve hours on a 12,000 mile tow, requiring us to sail in the middle of the night, 'oil patch' mentality.

We sailed at daylight on July 3rd and a few days later struck very bad weather in the Western Approaches. We were double towing with the *Tasman Zee* (526 gross tons, built 1958). In the middle of the night the mate let the tug fall off course and fouled the other tug's tow wire. Fortunately we were able to hold on whilst *Tasman Zee* had to slip her gear. The *Mississippi* (674 gross, built 1960) was despatched to assist and San Juan, Porto Rico was reached on July 31st after a tow of 4,000 miles. From there the tow was taken over by the tug *Witte Zee* (1,539 gross tons, built 1966) and we were sent off to New York.

At Newark, New Jersey we picked up the *Indonesian Star*, an 8,000 ton deadweight 1944 built Victory type ship fully loaded with scrap for towage to Cadiz in Spain. Once again the crew played up in New York and I had several visits from the police and when we sailed, two of the crew remained in hospital. A few days after sailing we got caught up in the remains of a hurricane, which had recurved out to sea off the US east coast. The weather was behind us and the tow was yawing uncontrollably putting great strain on the towing gear. Over a period of three hours, tug and tow were very carefully swung through 180 degrees and for the next five days we bobbed up and down in the one place steaming slow ahead.

Three runners were carried aboard and during the voyage they flooded the after peak tank to obtain a better towing trim and by the means of bottle screws, the rudder could be adjusted a few degrees to one side to stop the tow from yawing. After steaming 3,400 miles in twenty-eight days the tow was safely delivered.

Next stop was a light ship run back to Southampton, where I was relieved and proceeded on leave. All in all it had not been a very good trip, I was very disappointed with the crew and their lack of experience, plus the fact I saw far too many policemen as just about every port as I was bailing them out of gaol. The pay on board the tugs was not good and conditions aboard were very primitive. Unless the crews were dedicated to the life, and only a few of them were, they usually only remained for a single voyage. My wages as master were 220 pounds a month plus six pence per mile towing bonus and you earned every penny. My next voyage was to be my last with Overseas Towage and Salvage and crew problems were my sole reason for leaving.

After my leave I was flown out to Nassau in the Bahamas to pick up the *Salvonia*, a sister ship to *Neptunia* but two years younger having been built in 1951. The chief engineer and myself flew out to take over and the new crew followed two days later. Once again only myself, the chief, the sparks and second mate had ever sailed on tugs before.

We had our first call out days after arriving when we went to the aid of the *Velutina*, a 30,000 ton Shell Tanker but our assistance was not required. Salvage station was then transferred to St George, Bermuda which proved to be a top spot, a nice quiet place with some good runs ashore. The day after arrival we were off again, this time to the *Esso Australia* a 26,000 ton tanker, once again our assistance was not required and back to Bermuda we went.

Our third call out for that trip was the *Vainqueur Jose*, a 7,000 ton scrap ship fully loaded, broken down some 350 miles to the southwest of Bermuda. We picked her up in a force eight gale with a thirty-foot sea and swell running. She was two feet down by the head and her rudder was jammed hard to port. As a result she towed like a real pig. I reported our situation to London and they arranged for a more powerful tug to take over from us. After five days at three knots, we were met by Smit's *Schelde* off Mona passage, we towed together until the casualty was clear to the north of the passage and the weather had improved. After slipping the tow we managed to go alongside to transfer food, fresh water and fuel for his emergency generator. We returned to Bermuda whilst the *Schelde* continued on with the tow.

Although rated at 2,000 horse power, our actual horsepower was about 1200 and I think that quite a few of those may have died of old age and overwork, and the next tow was to prove this theory beyond doubt. The tug was ordered to proceed to Orange in Texas to pick up a swamp drilling rig and take it to West Africa. We secured alongside the shipyard where the *Lutuce* had just completed building. She was a big lump of a thing and although only drawing eight feet of water, her terrific windage was to prove a nightmare.

Christmas was spent in Orange and it was quite a memorable one at that. Christmas morning I was lying in my bunk when the shipyard watchman knocked on the door saying I was wanted on the phone. Upon arriving at the gatehouse, I picked up the phone and was wished a Merry Christmas by the local chief of police who inquired about the health of the crew. When I said I had not seen them this morning, he said that I wouldn't as he had them all locked up. True enough, going back aboard myself and the sparks were the only two remaining, the police chief had scored a baker's dozen: the remaining thirteen were in gaol.

I did not have too much cash aboard and being Christmas Day, the agent could not scrape up much more. We managed to bail four of the crew, including the cook but the others had to remain in until we could raise the bail money. The chief was an old rogue, but said it would be ok if we brought up their Christmas dinner, and if I also brought two cases of beer he would see that the crew got one. I think that the fine and bail money was about US\$ 120 each, which was just about a month's wages for a seaman.

Nobody was sorry when we sailed with our tow on New Year's Eve. Soon after sailing, severe northerly weather was encountered and our speed dropped dramatically. Our next problem soon arose however, that time it was generator trouble and necessitated a diversion to the island of Barbados where we anchored on January 25th 1970. So far we had covered 2,350 miles at an average speed of 3.9 knots.

Our eight days anchored off Barbados were not without problems. The tow ranged up against our stern doing some damage and a fire started in our forward store through old and worn electrical wiring. We topped up bunkers, water and provisions and with all three generators now working, the anchor was weighed and the tow proceeded towards our far-off destination.

Within a week the weather had turned nasty again and speed was down to two knots; we were also pushing an adverse current which I could not seem to lose. After about four weeks our new cook (never been to sea before) said we were nearly out of tucker, so in the year 1970 rationing commenced and the grumbling began in earnest. On day 30 things started to improve, speed was up to over five knots and we headed further north to Abidjan on the Ivory Coast, where it had been arranged for food stores to be brought out to us. We stopped for five hours off that port on March 6th and after a lot of hassle, managed to obtain enough provisions to see us to our destination.

On March 16th we arrived off the river entrance. There was no sign of a pilot so the tow was shortened up and we proceeded in towards the breakwaters. Two miles off the entrance the main tow wire parted. Luckily we had a run crew aboard the rig, reconnection was made, and tug and tow made it safely inside the river entrance. We anchored for the night awaiting an army clearance to proceed further up river and our pilot turned up in a dugout canoe, wearing his pilot's lap-lap (but no cap).

We anchored off the town of Warri on May 18th. Our trip from Barbados of 4,200 miles had taken us forty-four days at an average speed of just under four knots. Immediately on arrival, half the crew were demanding to go ashore and see the doctor. I guess that they went armed with pockets full of money, as they came back with notes that read, "Unfit to work, must repatriate".

Up the creek without a paddle, or without a crew should I say. The mate, second engineer and two hands had skinned out, but we had orders to proceed to Freetown and I wasn't hanging around that place for any longer than I had to. We sailed with the second mate, the two remaining engineers and myself keeping watch.

On the way around the coast we were told to go into Freetown for bunkers and then to Lisbon for a crew change. However before arrival, orders were changed to proceed to Dakar, take bunkers and then escort the *Kong Haakon VII* to Lisbon. She was one of three super tankers that had suffered a massive explosion through tank washing in 1969/70, the others being the *Marpessa* which was totally lost, and the *Mactra*. We arrived at Dakar and the second mate and the cook skinned out with bribed doctor's certificates. We took on bunkers and I asked the bosun if he knew the Rules of the Road. With the uncertificated bosun promoted to watch keeper we sailed and I then spent about 18 hours a day on the bridge.

The *Kong Haakon VII* was about one day ahead of us and even with him steaming at a reduced speed we never caught up with him. At Lisbon the crew were paid off and on return to London I handed in my resignation.

While in the UK I decided to attend a diving course run at the Siebe Gorman works in Chessington in Surrey. It was a fairly basic course but I gained a recognised qualification and even managed to get in a dive using the old 'hard hat' gear, which was not part of the original course.

I had decided to stop in the UK for a while and after getting everything squared away with the company, I flew across to Jersey where I spent the next two and a half months. Booking into the *Jubilee Hotel*, I settled down to a life of leisure and a bed that was not forever trying to land me on the deck.

The *Jubilee Hotel* was a great place run by a young Irish couple. Once they learnt that I intended to stay awhile, they charged me a good room rate, gave me the run of the place and in return I helped out behind the bar and with other odd jobs. I also secured a part-time job driving a motor yacht for one of the island's very well off residents, but I was not really suited to driving rich men's toys. It was a good time, I drank lots of beer, met lots of lovely girls and made some real good friends.

After two and a half months, I decided that it was time to get back to work, so I rang a pal in Singapore who offered me a tugmaster's job working back in Vietnam. On the strength of his letter I flew out to Singapore, only to find that no job would be available with his company for some time to come. However at that time jobs were plentiful and after a few days I ventured into the world of the oil patch, driving a rig supply vessel the *Eastern Advocate*, a 2,300 hp American built boat. Thinking back, it was an absolute heap of garbage.

We worked out of Singapore tending the drill ship *Glomar Conception* which was my first experience of anchor handling the oilrig way. We were running anchors and delivering stores, fuel, water, cement, drill pipes, casing and anything else you could think of. I stayed there for over four months, ending up in Darwin. Rig boats were entirely different to tugs and the complete loss of independence was hard to take. You were always under orders from somebody, usually a ratbag Yank whose sole aim was to make the life of those on the supply boats as difficult as possible.

One night we had to make an urgent 800 mile run out of Darwin and return in order to pick up the toolpusher's golf clubs and stereo equipment. I was tired, the radar was out for the trip, and after spending all night on the bridge I told them none too politely where to put their job.

It was then back to Melbourne for a couple of months off and Christmas at home. At the beginning of 1971 I settled back to life in Australia. A pal offered me a job on his tug *Sprightly* which he had just purchased off the Royal Australian Navy. She was a wartime standard American vessel built in 1943 and at that stage was the only true deep-sea tug in the country. Of 650 gross tons, she was 143 feet in length, 2,000 hp and fitted with a towing winch.

A problem then arose with the Department of Trade and Industry who would not recognise my tugmaster FG certificate and imposed a limit of so many miles from the coast that I could operate within. This was typical government bureaucracy at work, refusing to recognise a British qualification just because they did not have an equivalent certificate in Australia. Anyway, as it happened, they let me take command of the *Sprightly* which was contracted to act as a weather ship to the east of Bass Strait for the offshore drilling rigs that were operating in the area. We did three weeks on, three weeks off stuck out in the middle of nowhere giving weather reports. It was an easy job and as she was an excellent sea boat, we had no worries keeping on station in all conditions. The pay was good and I managed to save a good deal which was to see me through the rest of the year.

After about three months, our contract was finished and the ship was replaced by an automatic weather buoy which we towed out and placed on location. As we approached the location with the buoy in tow, the buoy's mooring line was paid out to full scope before the anchors were slipped from our deck. The buoy was moored in 2,400 fathoms and before slipping, over 7 kilometres of towline had been streamed. In the days before satellite navigation, the position was fixed using the stars. I am pleased to say the buoy was moored within one mile of the designated position. It had been calculated that the anchors would take thirty-five minutes to reach bottom, so all in all it was not a bad effort.

The *Sprightly* was laid up in Geelong and I enrolled in the Royal Melbourne Institute of Technology to study for an Australian Master Foreign Going Certificate, which would put me right with the local authorities. This occupied the next five and a half months with a 45 minute tram ride to and from school each day, which was a bit hard to take on a cold Melbourne winter's morning. I was very lucky in having Captain Ian Clarke as instructor and he was a great help when he saw that I was having a bit of a struggle with some subjects. In January 1972, I successfully passed master and was free to take up any position on the Aussie coast.

First job was on the tug *Jaramac 34* (220 gross tons, built 1968) towing a pipe lay barge from Geelong to Singapore. I was engaged as mate for the delivery tow, which was a typical 'oil patch' operation with not even a spare tow wire on board. The 5,000 mile tow was uneventful with good weather for the entire passage. Luckily it was good weather, for carrying limited bunkers, the tug had to go alongside the barge to fuel up every week. Previously when working with Overseas Towage, we would often meet another of the company's tugs at sea and carry out a tug to tug, fuel and water transfer despite all of those tugs having a very large bunker capacity.

We were paid off in Singapore and while the rest of the crew flew back to Australia, I stayed on, taking command of the salvage ship *Salvanguard* which was about to sail for Bangladesh to conduct wreck clearance operations. The *Salvanguard* was a wartime built boom defence vessel (ex-*Barfoil*) that had been purchased from the Royal Navy. She was an oil-fired steamer of 850 ihp and carried a crew of 25, the only European aboard being myself. Our first job was to tow a barge load of salvage equipment to Chittagong and then proceed up river to lift two railway bridges. They had been blown up in the Independence War that had finished just weeks before our arrival.

All went well until the approaches to Chittagong had to be tackled. A minefield had been laid in the port approaches and the Russians had volunteered to buoy a channel through the minefield and then remove the mines. I received a long telegram giving details of the buoyed channel which should have given us a safe approach to the port. This information was carefully plotted on the chart and I was doubly careful, as in Singapore we had loaded five tons of blasting gelatine to be used in the wreck removal operations. This was now stowed down below, and if we had come into contact with a mine, there would be a bloody great bang and none aboard *Salvanguard* would know anything about it.

Our radar set was next to useless because the low lying foreshore was almost impossible to pick up. A fair set of morning star sights gave us an approximation of our whereabouts and we anxiously scanned the horizon for the Russian marker buoys. According to the telegram received, they were painted in various colours and numbered. It turned out that the buoys were largely un-numbered and were all the same colour of rust red. However, we made it without mishap and anchored off the Port of Chittagong after a 1600 mile tow from Singapore, feeling very much relieved.

A river pilot was embarked and soon we were heading up river to our first assignment. As if things weren't complicated enough, the pilot informed me that the maximum draft allowable in the river was eight feet. The *Salvanguard* drew exactly double that and had sixteen feet draft.

Going up river was not too bad, a heavy anchor was rigged forward and immediately we ran aground this was let go. There was nothing else for it but sit down with a coffee and within thirty minutes we were afloat again, the five to seven knot current scouring away the riverbed and setting us free. Up anchor and off we went again, sometimes for five miles, sometimes for 100 yards before running aground once again. It was a slow old haul up to Bhairab Bazaar where the King George VI railway bridge lay up-ended in the river. Our main job was to act as a depot ship for other units of the salvage fleet, to lay heavy moorings and to act as a pull barge using our two sets of 60 ton ground tackles. It took about four weeks to lift the three sections of the railway bridge, load each 460 ton section onto two flat top barges and moor the six barges safely in the river. The very strong river currents made the work that much more difficult, while living conditions aboard the steam *Salvanguard* with no such thing as air-conditioning was close to unbearable.

The next bridge on the list was the Hardinge Bridge, located some 150 miles to the west. Because of our draft, *Salvanguard* could not reach the next location and while the rest of the salvage fleet proceeded to the site, we carried out various surveys of sunken wrecks that were to be removed under another United Nation's contract.

It was then I discovered the joys of going downriver. On the way up I had drawn a series of mud maps, using the radar set and visual observations which I

Lifting damaged bridges in Bangladesh

thought may be of some future help when we came to travel downstream. We had a stern anchor rigged and manned continuously, and as soon as we hit the riverbed, the stern anchor would be let go in the hope that we would pull up before being swung beam on by the current.

One evening just before dark (daylight passages only) we hit and were immediately swung beam on and were pinned hard against the downriver bank. Soundings were taken and there was 14 feet of water on the downriver side, that is, we were two feet out of draft. Luckily one of our small tugs was working not too far away and I immediately called for assistance. He was due to arrive the following morning. An anchor was dropped fore and aft and there we remained overnight, unable to do anything to get ourselves clear.

On the arrival of the small tug, you could quite easily walk along the downriver side of the hull — the river had silted up fourteen feet overnight. Using the small tug, heavy anchors were run fore and aft and we managed to haul ourselves upriver and into deep water using our powerful steam salvage winches.

At another spot where we had grounded continuously on the way up, I anchored and spent a full day in the work boat buoying a channel, before attempting the passage. Next morning off we went, steering between the buoys laid the previous day. It was all to no avail, as no sooner had we gone 500 yards then we were aground again. All in all, the Megna River was not a nice place to work. The tug *Salvana* (my old command) was nearly lost when she grounded and rolled over to an alarming angle before coming free.

Others were not so lucky. The brand new coastal tug *Ocean Six* departed our location towing a lifting barge. She anchored the barge and was attempting to recover her towing gear, when the gear fouled the river bottom and the tug was swung beam on to the current. She capsized and sunk within seconds, taking several crew with her.

The heat, disease, bad food and foul water finally got to me after four months and I was flown back to Singapore with severe dysentery. I took the train north and spent two weeks at Penang recovering, living in air-conditioned comfort, eating good food and sleeping about fourteen hours a day. On reporting to the office I was instructed to return to Bangladesh to rejoin *Salvanguard*. When I refused, I was very reluctantly given command of the *Salvista*, but my popularity rating was not too high.

During the two months that I spent aboard *Salvista*, two vessels were refloated using ground tackle. They were the small Korean Tanker *Miyang No 7* (800 gross tons) from Beacon Number 1 in Singapore Strait and the loaded Indonesian Tanker *Windrati* (17,000 tons) from the outer bar of the Musi River, Sumatra.

The *Salvista* with a shallow draft of only six feet could get in very close to most grounded vessels. She would first drop two heavy salvage anchors over the bow attached to two powerful deck winches by 1,600 feet of 40 mm wires on individual winch drums. Next she would back up to the casualty and pass over the ends of two lengths of 48 mm wires to be made fast aboard, the other ends of which were made fast to the moving blocks of two sets of ground tackle on *Salvista's* foredeck. The bow wires were hauled in until all gear was set up tight, the forward winch would then be dogged and heaving would commence on the ground tackle winches. That way a total pull of 120 tons could be exerted on the casualty. There was no need to stopper off the tackles, as when they became 'two blocked' it was simply a matter of heaving on the anchor wires, slacking off the blocks and the *Salvista* would be heaved forward about 100 feet (the drift between the blocks). The process could be repeated as many times as required, each time dragging the casualty another 100 feet from her stranded position.

However, conditions aboard the *Salvista* were some of the most primitive I have ever encountered and the refusal of management to pay me some kind of accommodation allowance for living ashore, amongst other arguments, meant that once again it was time to move on.

Next came a delivery job on a small supply vessel, with a return trip Singapore to Bangladesh with explosives, and then it was back home again to Melbourne.

During 1973 it was back aboard the old *Sprightly*. She had come out of lay-up and had obtained a three-month survey contract for the CSIRO to operate in

Survey ship Sprightly

Tasmania. That was a pleasant change; we had a really good crew and it was nice to have somebody to talk to after months of sailing alone with a full Asiatic crew. The Tasmanian survey was interesting, we did a lot of 'rock hopping' and went to all kinds of out-of-the-way little bays and inlets carrying out seismic and bottom sampling work.

That job was the beginning of a long association with the Korevaar Family, who owned the *Sprightly*, and a better firm to work with one could never wish for. When the survey was completed we took the *Sprightly* back to Geelong and then to Launceston for dry-docking. Later the towing gear was removed and a major conversion carried out. Under the Korevaar banner, *Sprightly* spent the remainder of her days as a survey vessel and was never again used as a deep-sea tug as she was originally designed.

On the trip down to Launceston I took my 13-year-old nephew along for the ride. Young Brett was always very interested in what his two sea-going uncles were up to (my brother Frank at that time being a Melbourne pilot). The two weeks that he spent with me on that trip, even at such a tender age, helped him to make up his mind about his future career. I am proud to say that he is now sailing as master on the Australian coast.

Back in Geelong conversion to a full time survey vessel had got into full swing. The ship had obtained a long term charter from the CSIRO to conduct fisheries research and towards the end of the year we sailed for Fremantle to commence operations. John Korevaar had asked me to stay on, but full time survey work did not appeal greatly. I loaded the old landrover aboard the after deck of *Sprightly*, paid off in Fremantle and drove home across the Nullabor Plain with my old pal Keith Sharp, who had been with me as mate.

Early in 1974 the small rig supply vessel *San Pedro Strait* (331 gross tons, built 1968) had to be delivered from Cairns to Bahrein and I obtained the mate's position for the run. We had a fantastic run weather-wise and we did the 7,000 miles run at an average speed of ten-and-three-quarters knots.

Back in Melbourne I had my first taste of dredging, driving the old hopper barge *Amsterdam V* in the Yarra River during the construction of the container berth at Swanson Dock. Even though I returned to dredging years later, things did not improve and I still think that dredging is the most boring job ever invented.

The harbour master at Geelong who was a very good friend, rang me to say that their tug *Sir Roy Fidge* (297 gross tons, built 1968) was about to embark on a double tow to Western Australia and asked if I would like the job as towing master (officially mate). This sounded a lot more interesting than carrying mud down the Yarra River so I accepted his offer. The *Sir Roy Fidge* was basically a harbour tug with no towing winch so my experience on the *Salvana* came in very useful. Our tows were the Bucket Dredger *Victoria* and the Hopper Barge *AD 503*. The towing bollard had been beefed up and both tows were attached to this, the towing hook not being used. Using the knowledge gained double towing with the *Salvana*, Captain Hancox (senior) and myself worked out a towage plan and the actual towing gear required.

Once again we had a very successful trip, the weather across the Great Australian Bight was not the best, but the 15-day tow to Bunbury was completed at 4.2 knots, then back home to Geelong at 10 knots. Once again it was hoped that further towage work would come out of this contract, however to my knowledge the tug was solely engaged in harbour duties until she was sold out of service and proceeded to Hong Kong.

Within a fortnight of arriving home I was offered a delivery tow and took the *Austral Tide* (663 gross tons, built 1968) with a barge from Northern Australia to Singapore. On arrival at Singapore I was lucky enough to step straight on to a return delivery back to Australia.

So ended 1974, it had been a busy year and all achieved with work from home. During my time at home, I had become very interested in 'bush bashing' and had bought myself a new long wheelbase landrover. I spent quite a lot of time and money fitting the vehicle out to tackle trips further afield. It was a lot of fun and was to cause me to leave the sea for an extended period.

It all started at the start of March 1975, when two intrepid seafarers (brother Frank and myself) loaded up the 4WD and drove into the sunset. We only covered about 2,800 miles on this expedition, but as luck would have it, ended up in the opal-mining town of Andamooka in the far north of South Australia. We spent about a week there but in that short time the opal bug bit us both.

Returning back home to Melbourne I managed a month's relieving work as master on the *Tasman Tide*, working in the Bass Strait oil field. Apart from a couple of very short-term contracts that was to be the last time I went to sea for another four years.

Chapter 5

Dropping Out in Andamooka

I put the Melbourne house on the market shortly after that month on the *Tamsan Tide* and in May I headed back to Andamooka. I purchased a small semi-dugout in the town for $1,800 (two rooms, shower, and long drop dunny out the back) and started scratching about looking for my fortune.

A few months later when the Melbourne house was sold, I split the money with my sister and headed outback with a pocket full of money and great expectations. The night I arrived back in town, one of the old timers grabbed me in the pub and told me that it was quite ok for me to have a go, but "Whatever you do son, don't stay around until you are completely broke and haven't got the money to leave town".

I thought that this was strange advice and such a thing could never happen to me. How wrong I was. I often wonder what would have happened if I had never seen Andamooka? Would my life be any different today? Instead of dropping out for four years, if I had remained at sea would have I gotten further ahead? I will never know, what is done is done and you cannot turn back the clock.

Andamooka was a rough old town, life was hard and the people even harder. It was a real United Nations and if six blokes were sitting at the bar together, there would be six different nationalities. Still I managed to get on with most of them and for such a small place, it was quite amazing the number of single women that were hovering about looking for rich husbands.

After a while I teamed up with a German, Gerry Modei, and we worked together as partners for the whole of the time I was there. His wife worked in the general store and as far as I know, more than twenty-five years on they are still there, still working away and will probably remain for the rest of their days, with little to show for a lifetime of toil.

We were underground miners, as even then most of the mining was done on an open-cut method using bulldozers. We staked our claim, sunk a shaft 30 to 50 feet deep to the opal level and then tunnelled in until we found something, or just gave up and started all over again. We shifted countless tons of spoil in the four years but found very little opal.

In the summer months we would be down below at sunrise, then by about ten in the morning we would have to knock off because our air compressor on the surface was overheating. In winter it was better, but overall the heat was unbearable with blinding dust storms and it was not unusual for it to go for a full twelve months without a single drop of rain.

At other times we would get floods, with the main street six feet under water and the town cut off completely with no supplies or mail for weeks. Even the clay-pan airstrip would disappear under water and the flying doctor would be unable to land. On one such occasion, I loaded up the landrover with the local nursing sister and a critically ill patient lying on a stretcher in the back. It took us twelve hours to travel the 80 miles to Woomera and the nearest hospital over sand hills and flooded creeks. We drove all night but the patient died soon after we arrived at Woomera. To this day I do not know if it was the illness or my driving.

Day-to-day living was expensive and the prices for food, diesel fuel, explosives and beer were sky high, with the latter forming my greatest outlay. Out of working hours there was not much in the way of entertainment and the pub was the centre of all social life. The other source of entertainment, except movies once a week at the drive-in, was the Buffalo Lodge. I got myself very heavily involved with the lodge and apart from boozing, we rebuilt the hall and more or less took over running some form of social life for the townsfolk. There was weekly bingo, dances about once a month, cricket matches and with the money that was made, we supported the flying doctor and made enough money to send the local school kids away on a yearly trip. Not many of the people had much money, but they were generous with what they had and anyone who was genuinely down on their luck would always receive a helping hand.

It took me four years to go broke opal mining, and not for the want of trying. We worked hard, shifting thousands of tons of spoil for very little result. Occasionally we would strike it rich and I remember one day digging out $10000 in about ten minutes. I yelled out to Gerry who was working a couple of hundred feet away and very carefully we sifted through the level, then wrapping our spoils in a handkerchief we adjourned back to town and straight to the pub and spent the next two days celebrating. As a result of that find we remained working on our claim at Lunatic Hill for another three months burrowing like rabbits to try and find some more. In that time we found about another $500 worth and finally pulled out and sunk another shaft in a different location.

So life went on and slowly my bank balance was draining away. A group of us went on prospecting trips into untouched areas of the countryside, always looking but with no success. I would say that about one percent of miners made their fortune, five percent scratched a living and the remainder went broke. There were no secrets to the game, no magic formulae where to find the stuff, just a lot of hard work and plenty of luck.

Apart from one altercation with the law — a practical joke that went wrong which I never lived down — life was fairly peaceful. I fitted out my shack with all the comforts of home, had my old dog for company and had my collection of books. However, as the money started to run out, I sat at home of a night reading about the sea and wondering what the hell I was doing. By that time four years had passed.

One day my mining partner Gerry had gone off to Adelaide for a few weeks and I was at a loss, for it was impossible to work the claim by myself. One night in the pub one of the local girls who I knew quite well offered to come out and drive the winch of a day while I worked down below. Judy was a really nice girl and everything worked out well. Each day after work I would get a couple of bottles of

Andamooka — home on the range

beer and we would sit in her house yarning, until the beer was drunk and it was time to wander home. Judy used to buy the Australian newspaper that usually arrived about three days late and one day she spied an advertisement. She showed me the paper and I immediately drove into town for more beer.

The advert was for a tugmaster in the Port of Eden at $18,700 a year, which was a fortune to somebody stony-broke and who had earned about one quarter of that amount over the past four years. I was straight onto the owner, Graeme White over the telephone and told him I would be sending an application immediately. Giving him a brief run-down of my previous experience, he promised to hold the position until my written application was received. Within a week my application was successful and I started to get things in order.

One thing that had to be done was to try and get hold of some money; the old timer's warning had finally rung true and I was too broke to leave town. I picked one of the more successful opal miners in town and armed with a bag of good stones that represented my worldly wealth, I knocked on his door. He agreed to advance me $500 (with interest) if I left him the stones for security.

The day before leaving, Judy and myself were sitting in the pub at lunchtime when the police arrived. They promptly issued me with a summons, the charge was for causing a disturbance under the 'Peace be With You Sons Act, 1911–1979'. They knew of my intentions to leave town, so to prevent this they handcuffed Judy and myself together. That was at about midday and the charge was due to be heard at eight that evening in the pub. Needless to say, we remained in the pub all day and had to go everywhere together.

The more beer we drunk, the more visits had to be made to the toilet while locked together; it was quite an afternoon. The word had quickly spread around town and by eight o'clock the pub was packed. I think everybody in town had turned up. Finally the police arrived and the conditions of my release were read out to all and sundry:

1. *That the defendant be of good behaviour for one day*
2. *That the defendant shout the bar*
3. *That the defendant not leave the pub until he had a gut full of liquor*
4. *That the defendant return to Andamooka in good time.*

The key to the handcuffs was then auctioned off for the flying doctor service and we were finally set free. So ended my life as an opal miner, it had been a good experience, I had made a lot of very good mates and had left richer in experience if not in my wallet.

During the next couple of years I did return on a number of occasions, but once I had gotten myself settled I was too scared to go back. The bug never leaves you and the temptation was always there to sell up and go back for another try at making my fortune.

Chapter 6

Return to Life on the Edge

It was very doubtful that the landrover would make the distance to Eden, so I embarked on the long bus journey via Adelaide and Melbourne, arriving in Eden on the September 12th 1979.

The tug was the *EB Cane* (ex-*Sydney Cove*), built in the UK in 1956, 245 gross tons and 115 feet in length, powered by a 1,440 hp national diesel. With single screw variable pitch, she was not too bad to handle and proved herself to be a good sea boat. On arrival that night I camped on board until I could get organised with some permanent accommodation.

Next day I met with the crew and went for some steaming trials around the bay. Although I had been out of the game for quite some time, it was not long before I was settled in and the best part was that at the end of every week, a pay cheque was waiting. Within a few days I had handled my first woodchip carrier and first tanker. We used to average about fifty ships a year and in the off time, carried out general maintenance aboard the tug. Life was good and I soon had enough money together to go back to Andamooka, settle my debts and pick up the landrover and all my gear.

Soon after settling in, I talked to the boss about outside towage work. Since acquiring the vessel, some outside work had been carried out and now he was very keen to try to obtain more towing contracts. We worked together to get tug and equipment up to scratch for outside work which, I am pleased to say, was not long in coming. In the meantime the wheelhouse got a complete overhaul and I got busy on the after deck fitting dolly pins, recovery rollers and gog rings. How she managed handling the deep-sea gear before I do not know (with great difficulty, according to the crew). Towing gear was upgraded with new wires, shackles and polypropylene stretchers, and we were ready to go.

Our first contract was in February 1980 when we sailed to Albany to pick my old friend the bucket dredger *Victoria* together with the cutter suction dredge *Crocodile*. We towed on two separate lines consisting of chain bridle, fore-runner pennant, polypropylene stretcher, main tow wire and chafing pennant. *Crocodile* was first on 900 feet of gear and *Victoria* next on 1,400 feet. We had a good run across the Bight with the weather mostly astern and averaged 4.9 knots to Adelaide where the *Crocodile* was dropped off, and then 5.8 knots to Geelong to deliver the *Victoria*.

We were away from Eden for just over a month and received a great welcome home, *Chartercraft* had carried out a double tow and according to the boss the sky was the limit. We were all given time off and I went back to Andamooka in my brand new Toyota Landcruiser. The people there must have thought that I had won the lottery. An enjoyable week was spent amongst old friends, but I had the taste of salt water again and there were no regrets in heading back to Eden.

Our next outside job was not until September when we sailed to Botany Bay to pick up the derrick barge *Leyton Candec 1* for towage to Hobart. That time the weather was not so kind and we battled our way south at an average speed of four knots. One bad point with the old *EB Cane* was there was no access from the accommodation to the wheelhouse and one was lucky not to get soaked through with breaking seas and flying spray when going off and on watch, should the weather be bad.

On our return to Eden, we just had time to berth a chip boat and a tanker before we were on our way again. That time it was up to Newcastle to pick up the catamaran drilling barge *WH Gemini*. That was going to be a long trip around to Dampier in Western Australia. We left Newcastle on September 15th 1980 and headed north. The *Gemini* was not the most robust of vessels and had to be nursed in adverse weather conditions. That plus the fact that we were stemming the east coast current had our average speed down to four and a half knots for the run to Townsville, where we stopped off for bunkers.

The run up through the inside of the Barrier Reef was very pleasant although conditions inside the accommodation were a bit on the warm side. Before sailing I had been onto the boss for some canvas awnings, and just before sailing he shot up the road, grabbed a tarpaulin from the disposal shop and threw it aboard. This was rigged over the forecastle head, where we all used to sit in the heat of the day. Combined with the lines of washing strung out all over the place, it was a wonder that we were never reported as a refugee boat.

The Thursday Island pilot joined us in Townsville and the engineer kindly donated his cabin to Captain Foley. Luckily John Foley had a good sense of humour and I think that he quite enjoyed his voyage on the slow boat to Dampier. During the reef passage we shortened up the tow and lengthened it again after passing Thursday Island. I had rigged a recovery line especially for this purpose and we encountered no problems. After dropping the pilot our next stop was Darwin where we again entered for bunkers, fresh water and provisions. After a short stay we sailed for Dampier, arriving there on November 18th after 30 days towing over a distance of 3,440 miles. We had circumnavigated half of the continent, and headed south to complete our round Australia trip. With a short stay in Albany to top up bunkers, the *EB Cane* continued her way home across the Bight arriving back into Eden eight weeks after leaving.

The company had another tug in Eden, the *Greshanne* (ex-*Iron Cove*), built in 1964 and of 225 gross tons. When purchased, the owner of the company had converted her into a trawler. That had not worked out and she had been reconverted back to a tug. During the time the *EB Cane* was engaged in outside work, *Greshanne* took over the harbour work. In order for her to be accepted by the contractors, she had to undergo a bollard pull test and that meant taking her up to Sydney.

I was on the bridge, the engineer down below and the owner on deck with the man in charge of the test clock attached to the towing hook. I think when new her original bollard pull was 14 tons, that day the man wrote a ticket to say we had pulled 17.5 tons. I really don't know how that could be, maybe the results had something to do with a brown envelope changing hands, but that was only rumour.

My next outside job was on the *Greshanne*. She had accompanied the Sydney-Hobart yacht race as radio relay ship. The boss had wanted me to do the trip, but not having any great affinity with yachties I refused. Anyway after the race was over, the chief engineer Vic Krisenthal and myself flew down to Hobart to pick up the *Greshanne* to tow the barque *James Craig* back to Sydney. The entire crew had volunteered to do the voyage with no pay just to see a piece of maritime history safely delivered to her final resting place. We received a good send off from Hobart and with plenty of press coverage, I even scored a photograph and write-up in the Mercury. Also aboard was a television news cameraman, who disappeared at the first sign of bad weather and didn't resurface until we arrived in Eden, and missed his chance to get any good footage of our passage.

In Eden we had to wait for a few days so that our Sydney arrival coincided with a public holiday. The boss kept telling us that although we were not getting paid, the Maritime Museum was organizing the biggest and best party we were ever likely to see, in fact I think that he even mentioned something about burning virgins at the stake.

One sunny morning in January we entered Sydney Heads, the harbour was crowded with pleasure boats and they gave us a rousing welcome. Slipping the deep-sea gear, I lashed the *Greshanne* up alongside our charge and proudly steamed under the harbour bridge to the berth in Birkenhead. There were thousands of people present as we drew alongside, I could hear the Premier talking over the PA system, saying what a marvellous day it was for Sydney. We waited and waited all hoping that it would be a marvellous day for the tug crew as well. Eventually some bloke came along, said thank you and well done, and tossed a case of beer aboard. It was all over. We had had our moment of glory, so slowly we slipped away and tied up in Circular Quay outside the Governor's *Pleasure Hotel*.

The case of beer was soon demolished, so we locked up the tug and went ashore to have our own celebration. The following morning we sailed for Eden, stuff all the Sydney 'silver tails', we had done our bit and were happy that the old ship had arrived safely.

When we arrived at Eden, my mate Vic Krisenthal penned a verse and put in into the local paper. To this day I have never let him live it down.

> *You've heard of Drake and Nelson, those seamen of great name*
> *But living now in Eden is a man of equal fame*
> *His record is outstanding with him I've had a jug*
> *He hasn't lost a tow at sea, disagree, and you're a mug*
> *Now fame has come his way at last he's getting quite excited*
> *A TV star he thinks he is, who knows, he may be knighted*
> *But when this tow is over and he has come to earth*
> *Those TV men won't seek him out, but we all know his worth*
> *The pressmen will ignore him, no cheering or brass bands*
> *But we'll sail with him on any day because we're in Jolly good hands.*

It was back to work again, but after eighteen months the routine of harbour towage was beginning to wear a bit thin, and there was no further outside work forthcoming. I was well settled in to life in a small country town, the job was easy, the money was good, what more could a bloke want? I wanted a little more excitement in life and I still had not fulfilled my salvage ambitions. With this in mind I wrote to my old mate Captain David Hancox, who was now a director of Selco Salvage in Singapore.

David was very quick to reply, and offered me a position immediately. He also sent down details of some of the tugs that the company was now operating. Things had changed over the past few years and the size and horsepower of the tugs had increased dramatically. Selco appeared also to be concentrating more on the salvage side of the business, which was also more to my liking.

It only took a few days to pack up the flat and move all my junk around to a mate's place, and before I knew it I was winging my way back to Singapore. There was no tug waiting for me and instead I was really thrown into the deep end. Within twenty-four hours of arriving in Singapore, I was on a plane to Colombo with a team of divers to tackle my first salvage operation. The *Zeung San* was a North Korean 14,000 ton deadweight cargo vessel, which had run aground fully loaded off the south coast of Sri Lanka. She had grounded at full speed on a hard rock bottom and was severely damaged.

On arrival at Colombo airport our troubles began. Amongst my baggage were three portable VHF radios and it took about two hours of hard talking to convince the authorities that we were there to do a salvage job and not to overthrow the country. The local agent was on hand to meet us after we were finally allowed from the airport. Then it was a long and hair-raising mini-bus ride to the southern port of Galle, which was the closest point to the casualty. At two in the morning the divers and myself departed Galle on a leaky old wooden fishing boat. Where we were going I had no idea, I only hoped that the fishermen did.

Finally we arrived on location, the casualty was well aground and the Smit tug *Mississippi* (4,000 ihp, built 1960, 646 gross tons) was made fast and anchored offshore. The salvage was a joint Selco/Smit operation and my job was to act as salvage master. The *Zeung San* was not a pretty sight, she was down by the head and well aground forward. On closer examination the forepeak had been completely destroyed with nothing of the hull remaining under the 17 foot draft mark, number one hold was tidal and numbers two and three double bottom tanks open to the sea. The casualty was landing heavily on the rocks with the hull twisting, and the grinding of steel on hard rock clearly audible.

The *Mississippi* was attached to the casualty with two anchors down to stop her swinging and causing further damage. There were already some small splits in the after fuel tanks and the last thing that we wanted was any more damage in that area. Various problems now arose that could have resulted in the total loss of the vessel and it was only with a great deal of patience and diplomacy that we managed to keep on top of things. Being an ex-Polish vessel, all plans and stability information were in Polish which complicated the situation and the crew who spoke very little English were not helpful. The master was a nice bloke who spoke good English, however I was not allowed to speak with him alone. The three commissars always had to be present and any information I required about the ship had to be put through them for their approval. This was very annoying and a great waste of precious time with the vessel in such a precarious position.

Barges were ordered to transfer cargo but it would be several days before their arrival, so being a rather low value cargo I eventually obtained permission to commence dumping operations. In the meantime, air-blowing connections were connected to the fore peak tank and numbers two and three double bottom ballast tanks. The bagged cargo was dumped from numbers two and three tween decks as air was introduced into the damaged tanks to displace the seawater. Furthermore fuel oil was transferred aft from number five double bottoms and those tanks filled with salt water to improve trim and lessen the risk of pollution.

The vessel was finally refloated at 0300 hours on Tuesday March 3rd, towed into deep water and anchored. That morning orders were received to proceed to Colombo and not a moment too soon as the wind increased from the east with a moderate to heavy swell. The stern first tow to Colombo took nearly 24 hours with the casualty sheering badly at times. Our towing draft was 36 feet forward and 29 feet aft, with the forward draft being increased considerably with damaged plating hanging vertically below the hull. Upon arrival, cargo was transferred aft to try to improve trim and finally a week after arrival, Lloyds Open Form was terminated, and it was with great relief that I boarded the launch to go ashore.

Two days later my new command arrived in port, the tug *Salvanguard*. She was certainly different from her namesake, the old salvage ship that I had had in

The water level in number 1 hold of the Zeung San

Bangladesh. The *Salvanguard* was originally built as the *Alice L. Moran* for the famous American Moran Towing Company of New York. Built in 1966 she was a large tug of 1,167 gross tons, 212 feet length overall and powered by four EMD diesels producing 9,600 bhp. She had a free running speed of 17 knots and a bollard pull in excess of 100 tons, a far cry from the 850 ihp of my old *Salvanguard*.

Our first job was to tow the 10,000 ton barge *Selco Giant* from Colombo to Singapore, which was a good straightforward run and gave me a chance to get the feel of my new charge. Shortly after arrival we were despatched to the Java Sea where the 12,000 ton Panamanian cargo vessel *Heliotrope* was refloated from a reef to the north of Tanjong Priok, after partial cargo discharge.

In April 1981, we assisted in the refloating of the container ship *President Eisenhower* that had grounded at full speed in soft mud at the western end of the Singapore Strait. Containers were discharged from the fully laden vessel by floating crane to barges, and three tugs including *Salvanguard* managed to pull her free. We were only assisting in both those operations, but on the next job I was back on my own again and that's the way I liked it. If things went wrong I only had myself to blame, but that was preferable to taking orders from someone you did not know and who you may disagree with regarding the salvage plan.

The Indonesian vessel *Tri Sakti* had grounded on the South Laconia Shoal in the South China Sea and we were sent to attempt salvage. This is not a very nice area of the world, being poorly charted with appropriate warnings printed on the admiralty charts.

The casualty reported that she was aground over her full length and possibly holed. She was loaded with 8,000 tons of cement clinker and I visualised the world's biggest cement box sitting on the reef. We arrived some miles off the casualty late at night and established radio contact. As *Salvanguard* drew 23 feet of water, I took no chances and remained well clear until the following morning. We approached from the east with the sun astern which helped to sight any outlying dangers. The Zodiac boat was ahead of the tug taking soundings and reporting back by radio as we slowly crept within two cables of the casualty and anchored in 20 fathoms.

A thorough diving inspection was carried out and the hull appeared sound. The edge of the reef was marked with buoys and we moved in and re-anchored within 100 feet of the stern of the casualty. Towing gear was connected and the next high water a refloating attempt was tried without success. The following day a stern anchor was run from the casualty on 500 feet of wire but on the next refloating attempt, this anchor pulled straight home and although we managed to swing the ship through about five degrees, no astern movement was gained.

Barges and grabs were being dispatched from Singapore for cargo off-loading, however I felt that if I could transfer ballast, given a few more days and a bit of luck we would be able to refloat without further assistance. I assured head office that she was on soft coral and our refloating attempts were causing no damage to the ship. After seven days the *Tri Sakti* came free and was slowly towed into deep water.

The captain was happy, the Salvage Association Surveyor was happy, I was happy, but I don't think the office was too happy, for no sooner had we refloated than the tug and barge turned up to commence cargo discharge. A diving inspection revealed no hull damage and the LOF was terminated on April 22nd.

Orders were received to return to Singapore with the barge. It had been a busy three months since leaving Eden, but it was nice to be back in action again and I was full of enthusiasm for whatever lay ahead. After returning to Singapore the tug was lined up for a tow to Palawan in the Philippines, which turned out to be not the nicest of jobs. Looking back through my diary, I just wonder how I lasted the distance.

I was by myself on *Salvanguard* with a full Filipino crew and therefore nobody to sit down and yarn to. The food was good when it came aboard, but once it passed through the galley became inedible. The engineers were totally incompetent and to top it all off I had a broken ankle with my leg in plaster.

Our tow was the *FPSO II*, a converted tanker of length 270 metres with a 20 metre diameter mooring buoy welded on the after end. Her displacement for the tow was about 75,000 tons and a mob of crazy 'oil patch' Yanks were in charge.

We waited for ten days in Singapore before the tow was ready for sea. There was quite a problem in getting our towing gear aboard as the *FPSO II* had something like fifty feet of freeboard. Luckily *Salvanguard* was fitted with very efficient hydraulic deck crane and by ignoring the safe working load, the heavy tow chains and forerunner pennant were successfully landed on board. Then there were the usual problems regarding sailing time. I wanted an early morning start as I had a seventy mile tow to clear Horsburgh Light and the crowded shipping of the Singapore Strait. The Yanks wanted to sail in the middle of the night, but luckily the Salvage Association Surveyor was on my side and we got our daylight sailing.

Despite some main engine problems and burning more lubricating oil than fuel, we managed to tow at an average speed of five-and-a-half knots for the 1,400 mile tow. Later I worked out that we were putting out about 5,000 bhp or a little over half power, that was the last time the tug sailed without a proper engineer.

On arrival at the Cadlao oil field off Palawan nothing was ready (usual oil patch stuff-up), I went looking for a safe anchorage as the southwest monsoon was blowing quite strongly. A safe anchorage was found off the northeast coast of Palawan and for the next twelve hours we slowly steamed in towards shelter.

For a good hour before anchoring I was towing either dead slow or stop. Although we appeared to be making no headway through the water, when the tow's anchor was let go, there was very little chain left in the locker before pulling up. Normally you would have a stern tug to take the way off but that time we were on our own; luckily everything turned out for the best. We remained at anchor for the next three weeks but not without some drama. While at anchor, two typhoons passed to the north very close, both causing massive damage ashore. However, our luck held and tug and tow remained safe at anchor.

When it came time to place the vessel on location the mentality of the Yanks amazed me yet again. The reason that our anchorage was so secure was that we were surrounded by islands and reefs, but still the Yanks wanted to head out in the middle of the night. Naturally, I refused, and was not the most popular.

Finally we towed onto location, holding the massive vessel in place while anchor chains were connected to the after mooring buoy. Once secured, the towing gear was recovered and then it was demanded that we start shifting anchors. Luckily, I always insisted on having a copy of the towage contract aboard and no amount of bluffing could get me to shift from the letter of the contract. Additionally, the *Salvanguard* was a tug and not a rig supply boat equipped with an open stern and stern roller. We sailed for Labuan where I was more than pleased to see my relief, Keith Boulton, come aboard and I was on the flight to Singapore.

In Singapore the plaster was cut off my leg after eighty days and I flew home for a well-deserved rest. I had been away for 21 weeks during which time I had been involved with four ocean tows and four salvage operations; it had been a very busy time. The boss inquired where I could be contacted if they required me back early? My reply was that I would be touring the outback and not contactable.

The two month's leave went past quickly with time spent between Eden and Andamooka and towards the end of September 1981 I flew back to Singapore to join the *Salviscount*. *Salviscount* was the flagship of the fleet and a big vessel for a tug. Built in England in 1971 as the *Lloydsman*, she had an overall length of 265 feet and a gross tonnage of 2,040. Her single screw produced 16,000 ihp and to assist in handling she was also fitted with a 600 hp bow thruster.

Within a couple of days we attended the *Lian Hua Cheng* anchored in the Singapore Western Anchorage. This Chinese cargo vessel had suffered a massive explosion and was burning out of control. *Salviscount* went alongside to try and control the fire while the anchor chain was cut and the ship towed clear of the anchorage and run aground in a selected location clear of all other shipping. Looking down on the burning vessel from the bridge of *Salviscount* the force of the explosion was clearly visible. Sections of the steel hatch covers had landed on the monkey island and most of the derricks had just disappeared. Not knowing if or when the next bang would come, it was not very comfortable lying alongside with our fire monitors trying to control the flames.

When she had been run aground, the Port of Singapore fire tugs took over pouring hundreds of tons of water into the burning wreck. I was ordered to stand off and throughout the night further explosions occurred, while the hull plating glowed cherry red in the darkness. That could not really be described as a salvage job but it was a rather interesting experience.

The next couple of weeks we lay at anchor and I started to have a big clean up. The tug was a bit of a mess to say the least and I commenced stripping out all the stores of towing gear and salvage equipment. About ten tons of rubbish were sent ashore by barge, and slowly things started to sort themselves out. Luckily I had Dave Hancox ashore and through his efforts, I managed to build up a decent set of standardised salvage gear. Storage racks were built for the proper stowage of pumps, diving gear, fire fighting equipment, etc. and by the time I had finished, the tug was capable of tackling most situations.

The other good thing that had happened was that we had a proper engineer aboard. Mike White turned out to be the most capable engineer whom I ever sailed with, plus the fact that he brought with him many years of towing and salvage experience. If we had all Filipino Engineers aboard, there was no way the next few months would have turned out as successfully as the way they did.

Our next assignment was an oilrig tow, towing the newly launched *Zapata Heritage* down to location in the Java Sea. Weather was good and the tow went well, but once again what should have been a pleasant voyage was made quite unpleasant by the loud mouth, know-it-all Yanks in charge. At all hours of the day or night, I would be called to the bridge to answer stupid questions from the rig. Every time watches were changed on the rig, they demanded to speak with the captain requesting such gems of information as to how much wire we had out and what depth of water we were in.

On returning to Singapore we did not have long to wait for our next job. The *Khian Captain* was a 14,000 ton Greek cargo ship fully loaded with general cargo. She had an engine room fire and was abandoned and drifting in the northern Malacca Strait. Most of the crew had been rescued by another vessel and upon our arrival we came across one lifeboat near the drifting ship with seven survivors aboard. Amongst them was the captain and as soon as we had picked them up, I had him sign a Lloyd's Open Form. One must always get one's priorities right.

She was a five-hatch vessel with accommodation aft and clouds of black smoke were billowing from the after deckhouse. Fenders were lowered and we lashed up alongside with our stern towards the fire in case we had to leave in a hurry. Four fire hoses were rigged from the tug's salvage manifold and two fire parties kitted out with protective clothing and breathing apparatus. Dense choking smoke and intense heat made access difficult, and, as always, going aboard a strange ship for the first time you have to figure out the general lay-out just to know where you are going.

I figured out a plan to attack the fire from two fronts and instructed the fire parties accordingly. However, giving instructions is one thing, getting them carried out is another. After about an hour, with the crews using up BA sets faster than we could recharge them although no progress was being made, I gave up. Grabbing Mike the chief engineer, we both donned BA sets and telling the crew to back us up, headed down the engine room. Visibility was zero as step by step we worked our way downwards towards the heat of the fire, while two more hoses blanketed us with water spray from above. Finally we could make out flames and within another 15 minutes the fire was extinguished. We handed over to a back-up crew and staggered on deck with only a few minutes air left in our bottles.

After that it was another four hours of cooling down with water spray and pumping out the accumulated water from the engine room bilges. Upon inspection of the after bulkhead of number five hold, the paint had started to blister and if we had arrived an hour later, it was quite possible that the valuable general cargo would have been lost through heat transference causing it to ignite also. That could easily have resulted in the vessel becoming a Constructive Total Loss and the salved value falling to zero.

As it was I was very pleased with our efforts, some water damage had occurred to electrical installations in the engine room but the remainder of the ship and cargo were undamaged. After placing a run crew aboard for security, the casualty was towed to Singapore and anchored outside port limits. The termination to the LOF was signed on November 19th, the ship redelivered to her owners and I looked forward to a decent bonus.

When it was all over I took a good look around the casualty. She was a relatively new ship and well maintained; the whole thing should never have happened. The vessel was UMS (un-manned engine room space), the fire alarms had activated and all fire flaps and engine room doors closed, except one. All that needed to be done was for someone to access the steering gear flat from the afterdeck, close the door between steering flat and engine room, and then activate the bulk foam storage tanks in the steering flat to the engine room. This foam bank remained un-used, if I had known that such a system existed it would have saved us a lot of risk and time, but for the crew not to activate the system was pure negligence on their part. All I know is that it ended up costing owners lots of money, which should have been just a minor engine room fire.

Another interesting point about that case is that it dragged on for a number of years after the event with claims and counter-claims being presented by various parties. I had to give further evidence when the job was long forgotten. From my habit of retaining original reports, diaries and photographs, I was successfully able do so.

On December 2nd 1981, we received orders to proceed to Port Hedland in Western Australia to assist with the *Co-op Marine*, a bulk carrier loaded with

115,000 tons of iron ore. However this was not to be and one day after sailing we were diverted to Bawean Island in the Java Sea to attend to a much smaller casualty, the 500 ton Japanese freezer vessel *Yachiyo Maru 26*. She had run aground on soft coral at full speed and was high and dry. Bawean Island was my idea of a tropical paradise, totally unspoilt with white beaches, palm trees and thatched hut villages. There was no electrical power on the island and I think that there was only the one motor vehicle, this idea of mine later caused problems with head office.

After we had cleared in with the local authorities, the tug was anchored off the casualty and a full sounding survey was carried out in the area. The *Salviscount* had a maximum draft of twenty-six feet, which was a lot for a tug, and whenever we approached a ship aground great care had to be taken. The Zodiac was equipped with a portable echo sounder and all rock outcrops and reef edges were marked with buoys before the tug was brought in to connect up.

The weather was not good with a force six onshore wind and heavy rain squalls. On the following day the towing gear was connected, but as soon as weight was applied various deck fittings were ripped out of the casualty. The next day was spent re-rigging the gear with wires around Samson posts and other strong points, making use of back-up wires and carpenter stoppers. Fuel was transferred to alter her trim and all ballast discharged.

It took eight days waiting on spring tides before the vessel was refloated. Head office advised me to dump 130 tons of diesel fuel from the casualty to refloat. This was before the word pollution was so freely bandied about and maybe I could have gotten away with it, but such action would have ruined the reef and fishing grounds and I did not fancy spending a prolonged holiday in an Indonesian gaol. Eventually the height of the tide was such that she refloated without damage. A quick diving inspection of the hull revealed no damage. A very relieved master signed the LOF termination and we returned to Singapore.

Back in Singapore work continued in trying to get the tug up to scratch and loading more salvage equipment. Things had improved dramatically since joining three months before, but I was still not 100% happy with the gear we carried and was forever trying to update and improve our salvage capability.

Christmas 1981 saw us anchored in Singapore. Two other tugs of the fleet in port lashed alongside for the day, and we were even honoured by a visit from some of the shore staff. A good day was had by all, a fair amount of booze consumed and on Boxing Day, myself and the Chief were not in the best of health. Unfortunately we did not get much time to recover for that night we sailed for another casualty that was to prove to be a long and frustrating operation.

Salviscount was lying in the West Jurong Anchorage when we were instructed to proceed immediately to render assistance to the cargo vessel *Roga* in the Gasper

Strait. *Salvanguard* was lying in the Eastern Anchorage, which was some four hours closer and upon sailing I queried the office why she had not been despatched instead. I was informed we were going because I "was an Australian". This strange response made sense much later.

We sailed at 2000 hours on December 26th to the *Roga*, a 10,000 ton deadweight cargo ship with Panama Registry but owned by the Israelis. She had run aground in the northern approaches to the Gasper Strait. At 2200 hours a distress call was received from the casualty saying that she was sinking and they were about to abandon ship. *Salvanguard* was cranked up to 16 knots and we sped through the night not knowing what we would find on arrival. On the run down I received a message from Singapore with information that the ship was fully loaded with bulk potash, and some undisclosed "sensitive" cargo.

To further complicate things a message was received from Djakarta Radio saying that the vessel had sunk. However at eight in the morning I had radio contact with the master who together with his crew, were now aboard the Polish vessel *Norwind* which was standing by the casualty. The salvage tug *Smit Singapore* had left some hours after us and I was instructed that if I was unable to handle the job, then Smits should be taken aboard as co-salvors. That was the last thing I wanted, but we kept going and prepared for any emergency.

At 2100 hours we lashed alongside the casualty. All of our watertight doors were closed and fire axes were placed ready at our mooring lines in case we had to leave in a hurry. The vessel had drifted clear of the reef and was anchored in deep water. She was well down by the head with a five degree list and it looked as though she would have taken the plunge to the bottom any minute. Upon our arrival the captain and officers returned to the casualty, requesting to land some "personal effects" aboard the tug, whilst the chief engineer and myself climbed aboard for a quick inspection. Ten minutes later we sat in my cabin comparing notes and I signed the Lloyds Open Form with the master. Our afterdeck was littered with the "personal effects" from the casualty, not one suitcase in sight but enough armaments to start World War 3. There was no way that that ship was ever going to be hijacked or bothered by pirates.

She was fully loaded with bulk cargo down below, while the deck was covered with containers. Hatch numbers two and five were tidal and most of the double bottom tanks were open to the sea. The engine room was also flooding, so all in all there was not very much keeping the ship afloat. We had to act fast: a salvage generator, diesel air compressor, electric submersible, diesel and air pumps were landed aboard. Air blowing connections were prepared and fitted to double bottom tank ventilators and divers put over the side to make a preliminary damage survey. Our main priority was the engine room, damaged pipes were plugged and pumping commenced. The casualty generators were still running and it was essential that we did not lose power. By three the following morning the engine room was dry and only intermittent pumping was necessary. Meanwhile pumping continued in numbers two and five hatches with some progress being made. Airlines were rigged and air was forced into the damaged double bottom tanks which in turn displaced the seawater through the bottom damage. That resulted in a large buoyancy gain and the initial danger period had passed.

The *Smit Singapore,* which had arrived on location, was informed that his assistance would not be required. I had been on my feet for 48 hours, but being able to tell the opposition over the radio that they were not wanted was like a real tonic and I was ready for another 48 hours.

As we were at a fairly exposed location with a six foot swell running, I decided to head for some shelter to enable the divers to carry out underwater patching. Towing gear was made fast to the stern of the casualty and at 1300 hours on Tuesday December 29th we were on our way towards the southern end of the Rhio Strait. Our chief engineer Mike remained aboard the casualty with a salvage crew to continue pumping the holds and to keep air pressure in the damaged double bottom tanks. Towing at an easy five knots we arrived at our new anchorage position late in the afternoon of December 31st. In the meantime, the tug *Salvain*

Roga *under tow stern first*

(300 gross tons, built 1972) had arrived on site towing a flat top barge with extra equipment and a second diving team.

Pumping continued throughout the night, however we were not making much progress and water was beginning to appear in number three hold, plus the fact that heavy black fuel oil was starting to show up everywhere it shouldn't. Now that we were in calm water, the divers made a thorough inspection and underwater patching commenced. Cracks were plugged with softwood wedges and then covered with epoxy sealing compound, while larger holes were covered with heavy marine ply held in place with hook bolts and sealed with epoxy compound. Within a couple of days the water levels in the two flooded holds were pumped down, a mixture of seawater and dissolved cargo being pumped overboard.

Meanwhile the containers, most of which were empty, were discharged onto the barge using the casualty derricks. However there were two full containers on deck and herein lay the mystery. Selco had advised that she was carrying explosives and when questioned, the master denied all knowledge of what they contained and said he had no manifest. I instructed the bosun to get a set of bolt cutters and open the two offending boxes and then miraculously the master turned up with the manifest.

The original story was that the *Roga* had cleared Singapore for Japan and had somehow grounded on a reef some 200 miles south of her course. The master stated that they were bound *for* Australia, although some of the crew stated that they had come *from* Australia. Even though it is now twenty years after the incident, I will not go into too much detail. To my seaman's eye the cargo of potash looked as though it was well travelled and had been aboard the vessel for a number of years. The containers were the real cargo and what had been in the empty ones I hazard to guess. The two full containers were packed with Mirage jet fighter spares and rockets (from a friendly Australian Government?) and who knows what had been off-loaded in Australia in return.

Anyway, back to the salvage. Permission had been obtained to dump all damaged cargo overboard to enable us to locate and seal all damage before towing the vessel to Singapore and redelivery to owners. Cargo grabs had arrived on the barge and those were rigged to derricks over numbers 2 and 5 hatches. Dumping of damaged cargo commenced by jetting and pumping of the soluble cargo from these two hatches as well. Heavy fuel oil was leaking into the lower holds from splits in the tank tops. Those were plugged and we got through 7,000 litres of oil dispersant to break up the heavy oil before the holds could be pumped dry. Steel patches were welded over the bilge brackets in way of leaks and extensive use was made of cement boxes: all time consuming and all hard work.

As there had been some leakage into number three hold, the owner requested discharge and once again grabs were rigged and jetting and pumping began. All three cargo holds were completely discharged of bulk cargo and finally on January 6th, the towing gear was transferred to the bow of the casualty and we sailed for Singapore, anchoring outside port limits the following day.

To enable the casualty to enter port limits there was still a lot of work to do and it was another five days until the job was completed and finally we were able to say farewell to the *Roga* and go to our anchorage at West Jurong. It had been a very busy twenty days since we sailed, but I reckoned we had done a damn good job and as it turned out the company thought the same. The only ones who were not pleased were the owners, I think that it would have suited them better if the ship had sunk in deep water and the whole affair could have been forgotten.

After writing out my salvage report, Mick and myself went ashore to the office to report. I was confronted there by Mr Kahlenberg, managing director of Selco and the major shareholder of the company. He informed me that he intended to visit the tug at the weekend, made no mention of the salvage job and just asked if the tug was clean. When I replied in the negative Mr K told me to clean it up. As soon as I returned aboard, the crew were put to work to make everything spick and span. I did not know it at the time, but that was to be the start of a long association with Mr K. My biggest problem in life is that I cannot abide bullshit and I tell things as they are, not as someone else wants to hear them. Maybe because Mr K was surrounded by a crowd of yes-men is why he took a shine to me. We used to have many good-natured arguments from that day, but in the end he turned out to be a really good man for whom I held the greatest respect.

To finish off the story of the *Roga*, a few weeks later I arrived at Sydney Airport on my way home for a spot of leave. For the first time ever I was pulled in by Customs for a baggage search. I started shaking and just knew that they would find a couple of kilos of heroin in my suitcase, with orders that if I did not want to spend several years in gaol, I should keep my mouth shut about the whole affair. Thankfully, that never happened.

Our next job was the towage of the new jack-up rig *Harvey M. Ward* from Singapore to Brunei. I shuddered at the thought, remembering the hassles we had on our last rig tow with my American friends. Talk about chalk and cheese! Although this rig was the exact same model as *Zapata Heritage*, Canadians were in charge of that operation and a more pleasant and amiable mob of blokes you could not wish to meet. The 700 mile tow went off without a hitch with not a cross word spoken and on arrival I was almost sorry to hand over to my relief Captain Keith Bolton.

Once again it had been a long hard trip with two commercial tows and two salvage operations, my salvage knowledge was growing by the day and I was the only master in the company who wasn't lumbered with a salvage officer during operations.

Chapter 7
Salvage and Delivery Tows

It was nice to return home to Eden and I decided that I would not be shifting very far in the future, so with those thoughts in mind I paid a visit to the local estate agent. Within a week of arriving home I had purchased an old fibro-cement cottage close to the centre of town and the whole of my leave was spent working on the new house.

When it was time to go back to work again, myself, my book collection and old black dog had a place to call home. At the end of two months it was back on the plane to Singapore, overnight there and across to Brunei the following morning to rejoin my old command, the *Salvanguard*. Our first job was to tow the jack-up oilrig *Chris Seager* back to Singapore, we had good weather and the 680 mile tow was without incident. Within a week we were called to assist in the refloating of the small Indonesian cargo vessel *Brastagi* which was grounded near Raffles Channel. That was a straightforward job and we were back at our usual anchorage the following day.

On the morning of April 28th, we sailed for the northern end of the Malacca Strait where the Panamanian cargo vessel *Carribean Nostalgia* (13,000 dwt tons) had been abandoned on fire. There were conflicting reports as to the location of the casualty and nothing was found at her last reported position. We were now off the coast of Thailand and I started searching amongst the off-lying islands. At 0740 hours the casualty was sighted ashore on Ko Ra Wi island, with smoke still pouring from her after accommodation block. She was ashore on Thai territory and as we had no salvage permit from the Thai Government, it was not the best of places to be.

The ship had drifted ashore in a rather awkward location, with reefs and shallow water surrounding the grounding position. We carried no large scale or reliable charts for the area and I had to be very careful not to risk the tug. While the tug remained safely offshore in deep water the chief engineer went aboard the casualty to try to access the situation. The ship was heavily aground over her entire length and no movement of the hull was felt in the two metre northwest swell. The accommodation was completely burnt out and large volumes of smoke were still coming from her engine room.

On contacting Singapore I was instructed to refloat at the next high water, but this was not going to be a simple hook on and pull off operation. Some preliminary soundings were taken from the Zodiac but because of deteriorating weather conditions, I decided to call a halt to the operation and we headed out to deep water for the night. The following morning further soundings were carried out with the edge of the reef and outlying dangers marked with buoys. Further inspection of the casualty revealed that she was flooded to sea level in the engine room and numbers four and five holds.

The *Salvanguard* only carried very light mooring anchors and as a strong current was running along the shoreline, I prepared for the golden rule, which is never connect a line to a stranded vessel without a good anchor down. If you don't do this and things go wrong, there is a fairly good chance that the tug will end up stranded along with the vessel you are trying to save. A four ton anchor together with a shackle of chain was rigged to 600 feet of heavy wire and this was readied for letting go from the tug. By the time all preparations were completed, darkness fell and the weather blew up, so off we went for another night drifting and safe in deep water.

The third day saw the anchor deployed and I was able to back up through the off-lying reefs in safety to connect up our towing gear. A thorough diving inspection was carried out and no signs of damage to the hull were observed. The water had to be getting in somewhere and my guess was a broken pipe in the engine room which had suffered extreme heat during the fire. We had no way of knowing which pipe and as all the sea intakes and overboard discharges were now underwater in the flooded engine room, we would have to patch from the outside. All sea intakes were patched with marine ply, epoxy and hook bolts, while all overboard discharges were plugged with soft wood plugs and epoxy. The tug remained connected to the casualty and anchored some way off.

Our next problem was that the tug could not go alongside the casualty to transfer equipment because of shallow water. Our three inch diesel pumps were too small to de-water the ship and our Zodiac was too small to carry across the large diesel salvage generator; what to do? Fortunately we did carry 3,000 feet of very heavy electrical cable, all we had to do was to float it across to the casualty. The tug was heaved back to within 1,400 feet, the closest we could safely lie and the electrical cable was attached to a 14" circumference polypropylene towing line, together with old life jackets, marker buoys, 44 gallon drums and anything else which would provide some buoyancy for the cable. The 4" and 6" electric submersible pumps were taken across by the Zodiac and our floating power line was towed across and connected up to a pump distributor box. A test run was made and everything worked.

The following day all patches were fitted and pumping began; almost immediately water levels started falling in all flooded spaces. However, a succession of telex messages from head office were not encouraging, telling us to get the ship refloated and to get out of there as soon as possible. That confirmed my theory that we did not have a Thai salvage permit, but in a case like that if you rush the job, you may as well walk away and leave it.

On the fourth day I roughly judged that we had pumped out sufficient water to refloat, the last of the fire had been extinguished and it was time to give it a go.

The anchor was slipped and buoyed, power cable disconnected and recovered and the tow winch paid out. Buoys marked the limit of safe water and during the refloating attempt, I had to be careful not to sheer the tug outside of the safe area. All our hard work paid off and at noon on the fifth day the casualty was pulled clear, then a five hour stern first tow to a sheltered position where her anchor was let go and the tug lashed up alongside. Our new anchorage position was also less likely to be visited by the Thai authorities, which provided an amount of relief. Work continued throughout the night and the following day. The tow gear was slipped from the stern and a chain bridle rigged forward. The salvage generator was placed aboard together with more pumps, rudder secured, another diving inspection, towing lights rigged, and anchor windlass wired to the generator. That night the crew had just about had it, so we remained at anchor and everybody managed to get a good night's sleep before sailing for Singapore the following morning.

Financially, it had not been a very successful operation for after delivery to Singapore the vessel was declared a constructive total loss and went for scrapping. To me it had been a good job, as I had tried something new, persevered and the wreck was salved under very difficult circumstances. The Salvage Association Surveyor must have put in a good report as several months later I received a positive response from the Association in the form of a nice letter from London.

Back in Singapore we remained on station with no commercial tows forthcoming. Once again, I spent my time working on the tug to improve her overall capability, including the fitting of a new Gyro compass and searchlight, which I purloined from another salvaged ship that was lying close by in the anchorage awaiting onward towage to the scrap yard.

Another problem encountered was with the Philippine crews. They were too used to good weather with no thought given that one day conditions may prove to be far from ideal. So another job carried out was the removal of all watertight doors and hatches, freeing up all the fastenings and renewing of rubber seals. I must have known something, as we were soon to need all the watertight integrity available.

After a month swinging around the pick we received orders to sail for Trincomalee in Sri Lanka for a ship called the *Blue Express* and assist our tug *Salveritas* which was attending. However we had just poked our nose into the Bay of Bengal when orders were changed to proceed to the *Donam Frontier*, a 17,000 ton Korean vessel fully loaded and broken down 100 miles west of Colombo.

The tug pushed through the steadily increasing southwest monsoon weather at 14 knots, burying herself beneath the sea and swell and I was very pleased with the work that had been done in Singapore prior to sailing regarding our watertight integrity. Five days after sailing we arrived at the casualty. She was fully loaded down to her marks and her decks were covered with railway wagons. The LOF was signed and the towing connection made even though weather conditions were severe. Our orders were to proceed to the west and deliver ship and cargo to her discharge port in the Mediterranean.

However, the orders kept changing with the possibility of returning to Colombo and it was a further twenty-four hours before confirmation was received to proceed to Djibouti. Knowing that the strength of the southwest monsoon would increase as we went further west, I asked for permission to put into the Maldive Islands in order to rig a stronger towing connection. Two days later we stopped, drifted in the lee of Tiladammati Atoll and lashed up alongside the casualty. A chain towing connection plus emergency tow gear were rigged on the casualty and after eight hours we headed west once again towards Djibouti. The run across was not too pleasant as the monsoon had increased to gale force with heavy sea and swell. Tug and tow rolled alarmingly at times as we were running with the weather more or less on the beam with a 30 to 40 foot combined sea and swell.

On the ninth day we reached Cape Guardafui and sheltered water. No damage had been done and all of the deck cargo aboard the casualty was still intact. Three days later we anchored the casualty off Djibouti and handed her over to the *Salvanquish* (6,000 hp, built 1967) for onward towage to her port of discharge. The next month was spent at Djibouti on salvage station and once we had settled in, it was not too bad a place to be based. We struck a friendship with the admiral in charge of the French Naval Base and as a result enjoyed quite a bit of hospitality from visiting war ships, including Poms and Kiwis. One evening we attended a grand cocktail party aboard HMS *Ajax* and HMNZ *Canterbury*. After sampling a couple of Pink Gins, I talked the steward into getting me a bottle of Navy issue rum and adjourned to *Canterbury* with Captain Carl and a few others for a very enjoyable night.

During that time we had two false alarms, once across to Mukallah in Southern Yemen for the *Maldive Image* which had grounded in the harbour with a full cargo of rice. She was a total loss and flooded throughout her full length so after a brief inspection and a report to head office, we returned to Djibouti. South Yemen was not the most pleasant of places, as we were given a hostile reception by the local authorities who thought I was British. Luckily things eased off a little when I explained that I was an Australian working for a Singapore company, but I sighed with relief when the anchor was raised and we sailed away from that place. The other false alarm was the time we sailed for the *Agean Wave*, a 10,000 ton Greek reefer ship fully loaded with frozen chooks, aground 650 miles to the north. On arrival the opposition had beaten us to it (Smits), and so once again it was back to Djibouti.

There was one more tow to do before my time was up and it worked out to be the worst tow that I have ever done in my entire career. The tow was the French jack-up rig *Ile D'Amsterdam* that was to be towed from the Mediterranean Sea to a location in the Red Sea. There was nothing wrong with the rig and it was a fair weather passage, but the job meant two transits of the Suez Canal and this I did not look forward to.

We anchored off Suez on August 4th and were promptly invaded by Port Officials who did their best to clean out the bonded stores locker. The following morning we joined the north bound convoy and proceeded through to Port Said where we waited a day to take on bunkers, and once again we were invaded and the bond locker took another hiding.

The rig was located not far from Port Said and on arrival I went aboard with the skippers of the two other tugs that would be towing with us for the southbound canal passage. The tugs were the *Smit Lloyd 43* and *Smit Lloyd 48*, both smart boats of 4,500 ihp. The two Dutch skippers were nice blokes and the Frenchman on the rig could not have been more helpful, in fact we enjoyed a very pleasant lunch aboard, and for the first time ever on an oilrig, lunch was washed down with a good helping of French wines.

Finally on August 9th, *Salvanguard* connected up as lead tug with the Smit Lloyds made fast on either side. Talk about a cast of thousands, this time we really were invaded and as skipper of the lead tug, I was the one who came in for the most attention. There were seven canal pilots in charge, one on each tug, two on the rig, and one each on the assisting harbour tugs. There was much yelling and shouting, but finally we convinced them that the three tugs should be lashed together for the transit and at least that way we were acting together and not trying to pull in three different directions at once. We were made to shorten up to such an extent that the situation became ridiculous. The propeller wash from the tugs was pushing directly against the bow of the rig and all we were doing was churning up lots of water, with consequent loss of speed and steering difficulties. As the speed dropped, the pilots demanded more power and the speed dropped further as our wash pushed the rig backwards while we tried to tow it forward. There was 21,000 ihp on that tow for a speed of about four knots and still the pilots would not listen, I managed to get the power knocked back, but no way were we allowed to lengthen the tow.

We had a few stops on the way and a change of pilots, when it started all over again. It took over 48 hours to reach Suez and then another change of pilots, they stayed long enough to grab their goodies from our sadly depleted bond locker, then were away long before we reached the entrance channel into Suez Bay. By that time I was just about dead on my feet, but managed to get the transport through the narrow channel without scuttling any more beacons and at two in the morning the Smit Lloyds were slipped and we continued down the Red Sea towards location.

The next day the rig jacked down on location and *Salvanguard* returned to Suez and dropped anchor. Keith Bolton arrived aboard on arrival and after a couple of quick beers, I was on my way ashore and booked into a run down hotel in Suez. The following day I travelled to Cairo by car, stayed overnight before catching the flight back to Singapore. Although I was just about at the end of my tether, I had to spend another week in Singapore with the company's London lawyer, going through salvage reports and preparing evidence for future arbitration.

Things were changing in Selco. Mr Kahlenberg was getting out and selling the company to Singaporean interests. The Chinese Mafia had taken over, especially in the accounts department and the Salvage Masters now had to report to a Chinese woman whose knowledge of tugs was non-existent. She was also very arrogant and full of stupid questions. There was also talk of salary cuts and that our four months on, two months off was to be changed to five on and two off.

It was time to make a move, it had been good experience while it had lasted, I had my name at the bottom of another nine Lloyds Open Forms and had saved enough money to pay off the house and get myself settled.

After leaving Selco it was to be another two years before I returned to the world of salvage. My first priority on getting home was to get my new house into order and to build some extensions. This kept me busy for quite a few months and I enjoyed the relaxed lifestyle back in small town Eden.

There was a fair amount of casual work available and as I was not interested in anything full time, this suited me down to the ground. I had done some relieving work in the Bass Strait oil field on two of Tidewater's vessels some years previously, and although not over keen on the oil patch, put my name down with Australian Offshore Services.

In June 1983 I flew to Singapore to pick up the *Grayvictor*, a 61 metre, 6,000 hp supply vessel for a six week relieving job as master on the northwest coast of Australia. Although only two years old, she had been laid up for some time and sadly neglected. The chief engineer and myself spent a few days trying to get her ready before the Aussie crew arrived and it was then I came back to earth with a thump, after the previous few years of working with Asian crews.

The crew joined one night, only to walk straight ashore again over some very minor complaint about the accommodation. Finally we loaded and sailed for Port Hedland and on the trip down, things started to go wrong. Main engine controls were out of balance, one shaft tunnel flooded, port side variable pitch gear failed, the air conditioner broke down and we had problems with our fuel purifiers and anchor windlass. To top it all off the boys put on a blue and demanded hard lying allowance as there were no tablecloths aboard.

On arrival at Port Hedland, the quarantine authorities condemned all our food supplies, a very expensive exercise. This was despite the fact that we had visited Hedland twice the whole voyage, once for inward clearance and the other for outward clearance. We only spent about three weeks on the coast attending the rig and then it was redelivery to Singapore.

On the way back to Singapore passing through Karimata Strait, the second mate sighted distress flares and we came up to a small Indonesian cargo vessel in a sinking condition. Weather was good so I managed to clamber aboard for a quick inspection. If I had been on a tug we could quite easily have saved her, but we had nothing aboard: not even a portable pump or diving gear or patching material.

The next day I diverted into Ketapang on the southwest coast of Borneo where we landed the rescued Indonesian crew ashore. We lost only a few hours steaming, and I knew that there would be all kinds of trouble and expense if we had tried to land them upon our arrival in Singapore. After redelivery everybody was paid off and sent home. I stayed a few days extra to look up a few old mates. It was very tempting to remain there in the hope of picking up something more to my liking but at the end of July I was back in Eden.

Less than a month later I received a call from Australian Offshore and on August 12th flew to Darwin to join the rig boat *Lady Sonia* as mate. If I had any doubts previously about the oil patch and they way they stuffed things up, that was to prove once and for all that all my theories were correct. Our job was to tow the jack-up rig *Key Biscayne* from her location off Darwin south to Fremantle. To carry out the tow, the 7,000 hp *Lady Sonia* was joined by the 7,000 hp *Atlas van Dieman*, both anchor-handling tug supply vessels.

Before the tow commenced, I expressed my concern to the skipper Robbie Anderson that our towing gear was not up to scratch. The nylon towing stretchers on both vessels were equipped only with soft eyes, that is to say no steel thimbles were fitted where the nylon joined the towing wires and I suggested that these would chafe through in a very short time. The towing chains from the rig were far too short, in poor condition and the fore-runner pennants were of insufficient length for re-connecting at sea. My other concerns were the length of the legs on the rig itself and that no emergency towing gear or recovery wires were rigged to the towing chains. However, the surveyor was happy with the set-up and as I was only aboard in the capacity of mate, I was politely told to mind my own business, as that was how things were done in the oil patch.

That the tow of a jack-up rig south to Fremantle should ever have been contemplated in mid-winter is highly debatable, given the weather conditions experienced off the coast of southwest Australia at that time of year. For the first week everything went well, the weather was perfect and the transport averaged nearly seven knots. On day eight, a southwest swell started to build up and that's when all the trouble began.

On that first night of less than perfect weather, both tugs parted the towing gear, or in our case the nylon stretcher parted with the *Atlas van Dieman* — the socket pulled off the end of the main tow wire. The following day saw both vessels reconnected and the tow continued down the coast. On the night of Sunday 28th, both nylon towing stretchers carried away again, the rig was adrift and before *Lady Sonia* could reconnect she had drifted from 23 miles to just 12 miles off the beach. Standing on the afterdeck of *Lady Sonia* with heavy seas rolling aboard, Robbie backed the tug down in horrific conditions to reconnect. The next thing some bright spark aboard the rig fired a line-throwing rocket at very close range; it sped down our deck and thankfully nobody was killed.

Throughout the following day a speed of four knots was made towards the south. During the night the wind increased to a full gale from the west and early the next morning our last nylon stretcher parted. The rig was rolling very heavily and had started to take on water and suffer structural damage. During the morning the decision was made to evacuate. The *Atlas van Dieman* remained connected while we launched an inflatable life raft and floated it down alongside the rig. But nobody was prepared to take the jump to safety and shortly after, the raft was cut free and drifted away in the mountainous seas.

During the day military and civilian helicopters evacuated all non-essential personnel, and I still marvel at the skill and bravery of those pilots in landing on the wildly gyrating helipad. The three jack-up legs, towering 300 feet into the air, were whipping through an arc of at least 60 degrees. How the choppers avoided those legs to land and take off with survivors was beyond belief.

Nine men were left aboard the rig but despite the best intentions on both sides, conditions at sea and aboard the rig made reconnection impossible. Just before dark the remaining crew were airlifted to safety and at about 1845 the final towline parted. Darkness had set in and showing no lights the rig soon disappeared into the blackness. Very soon afterwards she vanished from the radar screen so her final demise went unwitnessed and 48 hours later we steamed into Fremantle. That was my 82nd sea tow and was the first and only tow that got lost. A preliminary inquiry was conducted in Fremantle, but the threatened court case never materialised with an out-of-court settlement being made some time after.

The end of 1983 produced a couple of short term relief jobs as mate on the rig supply boats *Maersk Handler* and *Lady Sally* operating in the northwest coast. Aboard the *Lady Sally* the master was Captain Max Saunders, who is now a good friend and neighbour and holds the position of harbour master in the Port of Eden.

In April 1984 it was off to Launceston to join the *Lowland Raider*, a rig supply boat of 499 gross tons. Her job was to tow the 430-foot barge *Raymond S282* across the Pacific to New Orleans. The rig boat was British and the barge American. The Australian Unions demanded an Australian crew for the delivery voyage, so we took over from the British crew who in turn took over upon our arrival in New Orleans.

I was signed on as mate for my previous towing experience as the skipper was new to the towing game. The barge was empty and therefore very light and was rigged in the usual oil patch way. The chain bridle was attached to padeyes, although a perfectly good set of Smit's slips (albeit a little rusty) were lying unused. That time no nylon stretcher was used but a length of two-and-a-half inch chain was incorporated in the tow to add weight and catenary. Nylon stretchers were taboo after the *Key Biscayne* affair, not withstanding that all major towing companies throughout the world still use them with a great deal of success.

Our trip across the Pacific was quite a lot faster than the previous time and the twenty-six day passage to Tahiti averaged a speed of six knots. A short stopover for bunkers and then it was another twenty-nine days to the Panama Canal averaging nearly seven knots.

The weather was good most of the way and apart from trying to convince the skipper to try to pick up the Equatorial counter current, we had no problems. He, like so many others, thought that the shortest distance across the chart was also the fastest. However, tugs just like sailing ships of old must take advantage of any help Mother Nature can offer.

We towed through the canal and with the beam of the barge being 100 feet, it was a bit of a tight squeeze negotiating the 110 feet wide locks. After a further nine days we reached the mouth of the *Mississippi* where we handed our charge over to harbour tugs and proceeded up river to New Orleans. On arrival, the British crew were waiting to join and the Australian crew paid off and flown home. Our arrival coincided with the World Fair, so a few days were spent at New Orleans before flying back to the UK It was a number of years since I had been back there so an enjoyable two weeks were spent looking up old friends before flying back home to Australia. All in all it had been a very enjoyable voyage, a leisurely trip around the world and getting very well paid for it.

On the flight home I stopped off in Singapore to find out what was going on in the salvage world. I contacted Smits South East Asia manager and was offered a start in their organisation. I was also invited to a meeting with my old friend Mr Kahlenberg, who informed me that he was starting up a new salvage company and that he would like to have me on board. On my return to Eden I was buoyed by the prospect of starting up again and looked forward to what the future might bring.

Chapter 8
The *Intergulf*

Throughout September there were a lot of telephone calls to and from Singapore regarding the new venture. On September 26th I boarded the JAL flight to Tokyo before embarking on a five-hour trip on the bullet train down to Mihara on the Inland Sea, followed by a ferry across to the island of Setoda where the new tug was in dock for a refit. Mr Kahlenberg had sent two other people up about ten days before to view the vessel and it was now on their recommendation that I arrived on the scene to take the vessel over. The following morning I proceeded down to the dry dock to look over my new command.

What a heap of junk, I shook my head in disbelief that the *Ocean Bull* could have been given any consideration in the first place. The plan was to proceed direct to the Persian Gulf to take up salvage station, as at this time the Iran–Iraq war was in full swing with tankers being bombed and set on fire every other day.

I immediately conveyed my feelings to the others, I was the one that had to sail her and conduct successful salvage operations in those hostile waters and I demanded a half decent vessel with which to do so. Over the next two days, hours were spent inspecting her from truck to keel but my opinion did not change. I made copious notes and took lots of photographs and then telephoned Mr Kahlenberg in Singapore with my report. He was not a happy man as he had already paid a hefty deposit on the other's recommendations, and ordered me back to Singapore to report to him the next day. Back in Singapore Mr Kahlenberg agreed that the Japanese tug would not be suitable for our proposed plans and I started looking around Singapore to find something more suitable. I inspected another Japanese tug and a small Dutch tug. The latter, the 7,000 hp *Ijsland* of Willem Muller, would have been perfect had she been larger, and the purchase of her was kept as an option.

In the meantime my old pal Mick White had turned up to go chief engineer of our new vessel if ever we found one. Next Mr K suggested we go across to Bahrain as there were meant to be suitable vessels available. A couple of days later Mick and myself flew across to the Persian Gulf. There was nothing much there either, but a loose co-operation agreement was worked out with a local company so the trip had not been in vain. I flew back to Singapore while Mick White returned to the UK to have a look around Europe. Another week passed with no decisions being made, and further meetings were held with a Singaporean tug owner. I raised strong objections on the grounds that his tugs were completely unsuitable, but Mr K kept saying that I was too hard to please and he may have been right. Then word was received from Mick that he had found a tug in Germany. I spent many hours with Mr K discussing all of the options and finally the decision was made: go for the German tug.

It had been six weeks since I had left home but at last we were on the right track, I knew about German tugs and had always said that the Germans built the best salvage tugs in the world (my Dutch friends will not agree). Mr K asked me to fly over to Germany, check the vessel out and to give him a very full and detailed report before a final decision was made. On October 30th I took the evening flight to London. I met with Mick the next day; we took the plane to Bremen and drove down to *Bremerhaven* where the vessel was lying.

The first sight of the *Pacific* was just about enough to make my mind up. However not to seem too anxious we both spent two days inspecting the vessel before calling Mr K to tell him that the search was finally over. The *Pacific* was a beautiful tug. Although 22 years old, she had been very well maintained and just walking aboard you could feel that she was raring to go. I likened it to walking into a lost dog's home; she was locked up in the basin at *Bremerhaven* and was looking for a kind owner. She said 'If you take me, I promise that I will be faithful and won't let you down'.

Over 70 metres in length she was lean and powerful, her twin screws providing 6,600 bhp and capable of 80 tons bollard pull and an honest 16 knots. Capable of steaming 15,000 miles without refuelling, her raised forecastle towered above the wharf and I felt that she would have no problems in pushing through the wildest weather that the angry sea could muster against her. The more that I inspected the tug the more my mind was made up. The fully enclosed towing winch, heavy lift derrick, two solid work boats, large salvage hold, workshops, deck machinery and fire-fighting capability were just a few of the things that impressed me no end.

Intergulf (ex-Pacific) at Bremerhaven

I telephone Mr K in Singapore and received his approval to purchase the vessel and the following day we were placed in dry dock for an underwater inspection. Apart from some damaged plates she looked as good below the waterline as she did above. Repairs were put in hand: anchor chain ranged, new anodes fitted, water blasting and painting of the hull commenced.

After three weeks I was driven up to Hamburg with a representative of the owners. Taken into a VIP office at a large commercial bank we sat down making polite conversation and sipping cups of coffee. As I signed the cheque for her purchase I thought what my local bank manager would say, for that day was the one and only time in my life that my signature appeared for such an amount. It was just as well that it was Mr K's money behind the cheque for it was certainly well out of my range.

Even though the tug was extremely well equipped, during the next few weeks a lot of money was spent on extra equipment. A new satellite communication system was fitted, new radar set, new salvage and towing equipment, diving gear, safety and fire-fighting equipment and large zodiac inflatable. This list went on and on.

Christmas came and Mick and myself took a week off and went across to the UK, he headed home and I spent a White Christmas with old friends. In the meantime the Persian Gulf deal had fallen through with our newly acquired partners and our future plans were far from certain, but we had an excellent salvage tug to work with and we both looked forward to what the New Year would bring. Early in the New Year the Philippine crew arrived, it was well below freezing and snowing and I felt sorry for them coming straight from the tropics. As soon as they shifted aboard, the ship chandler took them all up to his store and fitted them out with cold weather gear. The next morning they all turned out in the gear in which they had arrived blue with cold — the new gear was too good to wear and they wanted to take it back home!

Finally on January 17th 1985 we sailed with orders to proceed to Gibraltar and remain there on salvage station. The Bay of Biscay lived up to its reputation and we punched our way through a southwest gale. The ship behaved well and a continuous radio watch was maintained in the hope of getting our first salvage job. Five days after sailing we received our first call and headed at full speed towards Setubal in Southern Portugal. The Turkish ship *Bora Isik* loaded with 7,000 tons of coal had grounded in the harbour entrance. Local tugs had tried to refloat her with no success, and we were instructed to offer salvage services.

On arrival the vessel was well aground and exposed to a five-metre swell making boat work rather difficult. Waves were breaking over the vessel but the master refused us permission to come aboard to conduct a salvage survey. It was not until four days had elapsed that agreement was reached and the Lloyd's form was signed. It appeared that the vessel was about 2,000 tons aground and most of her double bottom tanks were open to the sea. However, to show willing, the tug was connected up and a refloating attempt made at the next high water. Naturally, nothing happened.

Lashing up alongside the casualty, pumps and an air compressor were landed aboard and air-blowing connections made up and fitted to double bottom tanks. While this was going on I went ashore to try and organise a barge and heavy fenders to commence discharging cargo and fuel oil. This was quite a political operation and many hours were spent in sometimes-heated meetings with port officials and various other government departments. The magic word 'salvage' was thrown around at all of these meetings, and astronomical charges were levied under the mistaken belief we were going to make a fortune.

It was another five days before a fuel barge came alongside. We then managed to pump a lot of the fuel oil out of the vessel, preventing any risk of pollution. As the heating coils in the fuel tanks were not working, I took the calculated risk of pressurising the tanks with air to aid pumping and it worked! Finally, all risk of pollution was removed by discharging or transferring all bunker fuel, and my chances of ending up in a Portuguese gaol diminished dramatically.

On February 1st, the large Yokohama fenders arrived on site together with a very handy crane barge equipped with a fifteen-ton grab. In eight hours an estimated 3,000 tons of coal cargo had been discharged, damaged tanks were put under pressure and all intact ballast tanks discharged. The barge was slipped from alongside and the tug took up station ready for the refloating attempt. At 2100 hours we commenced heaving and by high water, the *Intergulf* was at full power and two hours later the vessel came free. The vessel was safely anchored and once again we made fast alongside.

There followed two more days of meetings, but by now the Salvage Association Surveyor had arrived from London which made the going a lot easier. Unfortunately this process of holding hours and hours of useless meetings — meetings that have no practical use in the salving of the vessel or preventing pollution but occur solely to justify the existence of a heap of shore side people — seems the norm today. On February 4th the release was signed for the Lloyds Open Form and we sailed for Gibraltar. There is a rather sad ending to that job, for on February 13th 1987, the *Bora Isik* sank in a North Atlantic gale with heavy loss of life.

Gibraltar was officially our home port as that was where we were then registered. For the next month we lay at Gibraltar, where there were several false alarms for salvage jobs and a succession of contract tows were put forward without result. Still it was a very pleasant place to lie on station and I managed to get a lot of maintenance work done both on the tug and on our portable salvage equipment. Mr K kept in regular touch from Singapore and it seemed that he was about to purchase another two tugs and I could see my dream job of marine superintendent/salvage master becoming a reality at long last; unfortunately that never happened.

Five weeks after arriving at Gibraltar we sailed for the Suez Canal. We had a rough old trip through the Med and two diversions before we reached the Canal on March 25th. It was straight through the canal and then to anchor off Suez to await further orders. I had been on the go for over six months and was anxious for a spot of leave. However, our orders changed by the day and after a week at anchor I was ordered to hand over to the mate and get back to Singapore for an urgent meeting with Mr K. There was still a strong possibility of proceeding to the war zone in the Persian Gulf, so my time in Suez was spent getting all the fire-fighting gear into top order and training the crew in its use.

In Singapore I interviewed an old mate Bob Nicholson with the hope that he would take over the tug, as I had very little faith in the mate whom I had left in charge. Mr K was happy with the way things were going and there was further talk of purchasing more tugs. He wished me a good leave and the next day I was on my way home.

A week after arriving home, the *Intergulf* landed a contract to tow a 60,000 ton tanker from Suez to Taiwan for scrap. I immediately rang Bob Nicholson back in the UK and luckily for me he agreed to take on the tow. I sat back to enjoy my holiday with my old pal David Hancox who had come up home to visit.

At six one morning the telephone rang. The *Woolongong* had gone ashore on Gabo Island, some 40 miles to the south of Eden and United Salvage had offered their services. By nine that morning we were on site at Gabo Island in a hired sharkcat. The vessel was hard aground on the southeast corner of the island, lying on a rocky bottom and very low in the water. The rig supply vessel *Swan Tide* was anchored close by and had earlier attempted to refloat the vessel, fortunately without success.

Once again the golden rule regarding ships aground had been broken. In 99% of strandings, the casualty should be pulled free in the exact opposite direction in which she grounded. By doing this much less damage is caused to the grounded vessel and the chance of a positive outcome is far greater. The *Swan Tide* had attached a towline to the bow of the casualty and tried to refloat, pulling at about ninety degrees to her grounded heading. All she had succeeded in doing was to cause further massive hull damage, and had she managed to pull the *Woolongong* free, it is certain that the vessel would have immediately foundered.

After a quick yarn with her commanding officer, we headed back to Eden to commence organising the various items of salvage equipment that would be required. In the meantime United Salvage was sourcing salvage equipment from far and wide, for in 1985 the amount of specialised salvage equipment available in Australia ranged from limited to non-existent.

Airbags were flown in from Suva and salvage pumps came down from a government store in Canberra. Those pumps were part of a government emergency response pool of equipment, but as they operated on 60 cycles and the generators that should have accompanied them had been sold off, they were just so much ballast. Apparently the public servants were unaware that Australia operates on 50 cycles and to obtain a suitable generator to drive their pumps, one would have to go to the USA and hire one there.

The Eden tug *Greshanne* (1,050 hp, built 1964) was prepared to assist in the salvage. Fortunately that tug had previously been used as a trawler and was equipped with a large winch. The refloating effort would require a steady pull as opposed to a heavy and violent jerk if further damage was not to be done to the lightly constructed casualty. At 1600 hours on May 2nd 1985 I sailed as skipper of the *Greshanne* towing the flat top barge *Emu* which was loaded down with salvage gear. At eight the following morning, the barge was anchored close to the casualty while a heavy anchor was rigged aboard the tug to hold her in position whilst winching. The tug's own anchors were very light and not capable of holding the tug in position against the pull of the winch.

An air compressor was rigged from the barge and Dave Hancox started pressurising various compartments to push the seawater out through the bottom

Baralga *loading railway sleepers, Eden, NSW*

Britonia *leaving Taranto with double tow*

RFA Typhoon *connecting to AFD 59*

Tug Neptunia *at Rotterdam after the long tow*
(courtesy of the National Tug Museum, Netherlands)

Lutuce *towing up river at Warri, West Africa*

James Craig *arriving at Sydney*

Steel and cement patches of cargo hold Roga

Yachiyo Maru 26 *ashore at Bawean Island*

Caribbean Nostalgia *ashore and burning*

HMAS Woolongong, *Gabo Island, Victoria*

Key Biscayne *nearing the end*

Tug Tasman Hauler *scuttled off Eden*

Daishowa Maru *ashore in Twofold Bay*

Master of the dredger, AM Vella

Trawler Lochiel *coming afloat*

Tug Pacific Salvor *alongside casualty*

Deck of Swissco *showing grapnel and diving spread*

Bosta Kayung *rigged for parbuckling...*

...and the right way up!

The Leuser *as found*

Cantilever arms and support beams in position

Lifting clear and slowly coming upright

World Discoverer *stranded at the Solomon Islands*

A very unhappy salvage master

Digging pits for log anchors

Tug Masthead *alongside* Ligaya

Refloating the Hanjin Dampier *in September 2002*
(courtesy of Wijsmuller Salvage)

hull damage. Air and petrol pumps were rigged and de-watering of sound compartments began. Because of the massive hull damage, eighty tons of air lifting bags were secured to the hull and inflated, whilst the tug kept a steady strain on the winch wire to prevent the casualty from moving further ashore as she was lightened. The winch wire was connected to the stern of the casualty as she was to be pulled off on a reciprocal heading when she drove ashore.

The casualty refloated at 2030 hours and was held in position until a thorough examination had been carried out and it was deemed safe to attempt to tow her the forty miles back to Eden. Towing gear was transferred to the bow and shortly after midnight, we very carefully proceeded to get underway. The weather was perfect but a weather front was approaching and strong to gale force southwest winds were forecast within 24 hours. At a speed of less than three knots we towed north up the coast, any greater speed would put an unacceptable strain on the airbags and at that stage they were the only things that were keeping the casualty afloat. After 14 hours we steamed into Twofold Bay and the casualty was safely secured to a mooring prior to being placed on the local slipway for temporary repairs.

The operation went off fairly well and although the final repair bill would have been extremely large, at least the vessel was saved together with a few of the taxpayer's dollars. The one thing that struck me with the whole job though, was the lack of availability of suitable salvage equipment and I made future plans to remedy that situation.

A week later, I was off back to Singapore for a week of meetings with Mr K and various other parties. While there I prepared a quotation to tow a barge from Japan to Wainwright in Alaska and return and kept my fingers crossed. That would mean a trip up through the Bering Strait and as the *Intergulf* was full Ice Class and built like a brick outhouse, it would have been quite an experience.

Then it was up to Hong Kong for another week where I had meetings with one of the well-known Offer brothers who were mates with Mr K, regarding ship management.

The *Intergulf* was due in Taiwan with the tanker *Hassan B* that she had towed across from Suez, so it was across to Koahsiung to take over the tug from Bob Nicholson. The day I joined we obtained an LOF on the tanker *Harris* (99,700 dwt tons) which was adrift in the South China Sea. Leaving Koahsiung we steamed to the east of Taiwan and straight into a typhoon. Despite the atrocious weather conditions we managed to get alongside and connect up the towing gear in a thirty foot sea and swell with the wind gusting between force 8 and 12, but not before suffering an amount of damage to our bulwarks and rubbing strake.

Getting away to stream the gear, solid green seas were rolling across the tow deck. It was dark with gale force winds and was not one of the nicest experiences I have enjoyed. However, one of the old tug's best points was that everything was controlled from the after bridge and none of the crew had to risk their lives on deck. During the night we barely made headway as I wanted a bit of daylight to see what was going on before applying any great power. We headed north and come daylight speed was increased until we were doing four-and-a-half knots. Across the top of Taiwan and south down the strait weather conditions became easier and life aboard a little more pleasant. Five days after leaving we anchored the casualty off Koahsiung from where we had started. She was going for scrap and one of the conditions of the sale was that she had to arrive under her own power.

The next few days were spent alongside the casualty providing water, spare parts and even steam from our salvage boiler to enable her to complete the last two miles of her final journey under her own power. It was a bloody awful job but it was quick and it paid well, so Mr K was happy. As soon as we were all finished it was off to Hong Kong to take up salvage station. Hong Kong was a good place to lie on station; we anchored in the inner harbour close by to everything and the best part was that we could only obtain a 48 hour open port clearance. That meant that every second day the chief engineer and myself went ashore to renew the clearance, so that we were always ready to depart should a salvage arise.

The first day there the tug was adopted by an elderly Chinese lady in her small houseboat. She remained with us continuously and provided our taxi service ashore. I spent a lot of time ashore doing the rounds of various offices. We were virtually unknown as salvors in the region and it was essential that people such as Lloyd's Agents, the Salvage Association, Average Adjusters and others in the local maritime community knew of our presence and what services we could offer.

A good social life was also enjoyed and as there was no work for the crew on Sunday, it became party day. About twenty Filipino maids, of whom there seemed to be thousands in Hong Kong, spent the day aboard with much music, singing and dancing until the small hours. The Philippine crew thought that this was great and as a result they turned out to be a very loyal bunch of lads.

Three weeks after arriving, I was called to the office of one of the Average Adjusters and asked how long it would take for the tug to put to sea. When I answered ten minutes, they were amazed and asked us to sail immediately for a small container ship which was on fire in the Taiwan Strait. We sailed immediately with no contract, however Mr K back in Singapore was trying to get a hold of the owners and was in constant touch with us. The *Formosa Container* was a 6,000 dwt container vessel, fully loaded, on fire and abandoned by her crew.

A few hours before arriving at the casualty I was informed that the ROC Navy had taken over the operation. We passed close by the casualty and offered our services to the Naval tug through our local agent, but our offer was declined. Feeling a bit despondent we watched the Naval tug stuffing about for a while and then proceeded a few miles to Keelung and anchored outside of port limits.

Formosa Container *arriving at Keelung*

A few hours later we received a visit from the local Salvage Association Surveyor asking us to take over as the Navy had put the operation into the too hard basket and had gone home. After agreeing to hire rates we sailed once again and made fast alongside the casualty at 2200 hours. She was anchored in a very strong current and still afire. We had lost twelve hours through the Navy's refusal to allow us to assist, and during that time the fire damage had almost rendered the vessel a total loss.

By morning, the fire had been extinguished, towing gear rigged and the rudder locked amidships. Permission was obtained to enter harbour and our tow was safely delivered to Keelung. It had only been a small job, but it helped to pay the bills for another month.

We left Keelung as soon as our charge had been delivered and went to anchor off the port. Another typhoon was approaching and after a couple of days the anchorage became untenable so I headed back to the Taiwan Strait to ride out the storm. Winds of 70 to 80 knots drove the spray so hard that the paint from the funnel was stripped, including the new large yellow K that had only been painted there days before.

After the weather had abated it was back to Keelung once again to await orders. Another six weeks were spent there, where there were a couple of false alarms with call outs to casualties that did not eventuate and contract tows that just did not happen. Our biggest problem was that we were an unknown entity in the towing and salvage world. Mr K insisted on working from home and we had no visible presence to the outside world, just this mysterious tug that happened to appear at odd times at various ports around South East Asia.

Time aboard was not wasted however. We carried a full time boilermaker, and with myself as unofficial ship's carpenter all the salvage stores and workshops were rebuilt with all salvage gear stowed in proper racks and shelves. Our extensive array of salvage equipment was properly stowed and fully maintained and the ship was painted throughout; we looked the part even though there was not much money coming in.

At the end of September my four months were up and Bob Nicholson and a new chief engineer joined and Mick and myself proceeded on our different ways to go home on leave. On the way home I spent a few days in Singapore with Mr K and it was agreed that I should start up K Salvage Company (Australia) Limited with the long term plan of setting up an independent salvor in this part of the world.

During my leave this was done and we nearly obtained our first job. The *Nella Dan* was fast in thick ice down in Antarctica and I gave the Antarctic Division in Hobart a price for sending the *Intergulf* down from Hong Kong. Before we had purchased her, the tug had been regularly used in the Baltic Sea for ice breaking by the previous owners. The Antarctic Division were very interested, however the weather eased and the *Nella Dan* managed to get herself free before the contract was signed.

K Salvage (Aust) Pty was incorporated in 1986 and I started buying in salvage equipment to handle small ship salvage operations. Every spare dollar was invested in equipment. (The venture failed in the end, but more about this later.) At the end of February it was back to Singapore, the tug had done very little in the time that I was at home. There was talk of going to the Persian Gulf, then more talk about going to Canada. We had no idea what the future held and Mr K was very indecisive.

Work continued on board the tug, including the complete overhaul of our two work boats and the fitting out of the carpenter's workshop. We finally received two large Yokohama fenders so we would not do any more damage the next time we lashed alongside a casualty in bad weather. We had lots of fire drills, with all the gear tested and the boys wearing fire suits and breathing gear, just in case we ended up in the middle of the Gulf War.

Mr K was very cagey, asking lots of questions but not giving out any information. One month after arriving in Singapore, disaster struck. Two gentlemen came aboard for an inspection and here all my devotion to duty came unstuck. They wandered over the tug for several hours with looks of amazement on their faces. The condition of the tug, the state of the towing gear, salvage stores, work boats, fire fighting gear and salvage equipment was just too much for them and they practically ran ashore with their cheque book, straight up to see Mr K.

The *Intergulf* had been sold from under me to International Marine Services in Dubai. The only thing that kept me sane was that Mr K had mentioned the idea of buying an old rig supply boat and fitting her out for salvage to be run by K Salvage Australia. In the end this was just another pipe dream as he soon forgot the idea in a very short time.

The trip across to Dubai was not a pleasant one, I had put my heart and soul into the old tug and all my good work was vanishing before my eyes. IMS were definitely not a salvage company, just a mob of opportunists who were going to cash in on the Gulf War. They made a token offer of employment at about half rate of pay with very limited leave conditions. When I declined their offer, I was treated like a leper and they could not get rid of me fast enough.

The day we closed ship's articles, they presented the entire crew with a termination letter to sign, saying that we held no further claim against the company. I read it carefully only to discover that we were being denied payment for our last two salvage jobs, which they had agreed to take over responsibility from Mr K. I made an amendment to the letter and instructed all the crew to do the same. Naturally IMS were furious but in the end payment was made. The crew were most anxious to know what I was going to do, and when they learnt that I was not staying, six of the senior hands also resigned and refused to sign new articles. My popularity with IMS sunk even lower. I was ordered to leave the tug and spend the next two days waiting for a flight on a barge moored miles away from town. I promptly ordered a taxi and moved up-town to a first class hotel.

Finally I left the Gulf on a flight back to Singapore for a final meeting with Mr K, before returning back home to Eden once again May 1986.

Chapter 9

A Mixed Bag

The rest of the year was taken up gathering more salvage equipment in Eden. This was quite an expensive exercise but I was still hoping for some financial support from Mr K, however this never happened. Towards the end of 1986, a firm in New Zealand approached me to take over a small container ship on a newly instigated Pacific Islands service. This was not really my cup of tea, but I agreed as there was also talk of the same firm buying the tug *Seefalke*, and to run this tug in the Pacific would have been most rewarding.

I joined the *Capricornia* in Wellington in mid-September. She was an ex-Union Steamship vessel of 3,068 gross tons and was in a fairly poor state, having been laid up for some time. This was my first job as master of a cargo ship and the thing that got me down the most, was the amount of paperwork involved. We sailed to Auckland to load and then around the Pacific, first Suva then on to Tonga, Apia, Pago Pago, Honolulu, then back. I did not mind the regular watches or the many extra hours on the bridge around the islands or the cargo work. But having to spend at least four hours every day doing heaps of paper work, a lot of it totally unnecessary, was the thing that made me leave the vessel on our arrival back in New Zealand.

I was lucky that we had no problems on that first trip, as her stability was rather dodgy. Some time later she rolled over and sank at the wharf in Suva, my mate Rainer Kasel from Singapore securing the wreck clearance contract.

During 1987 a couple of interesting jobs came up, but nothing in the towing and salvage line. To keep the wolf from the door I ended up driving the work boat in Eden tending the visiting tankers, but the first job for the year was a delivery contract of a small tug from Brisbane to Geelong. I gathered some mates from Eden and we flew up to Brisbane to take over the tug. Everything went ok until bad weather forced us to shelter in Eden. The telephone rang hot and I was in big strife with the Unions who wanted to put a cast of thousands aboard. Finally we were allowed to sail when another mate arrived. The trip down the coast was fairly rough and she was not a big vessel; the mate was seasick as soon as we left the wharf and did not surface until we sailed into Port Phillip Bay. So much for Union rules and regulations.

The salvage equipment was still building up and the new airbags had their first test on a local lifting job. Quotes were submitted for various small salvage operations around the coast but without success, lacking a suitable work boat was my biggest handicap and no way could I afford to purchase one.

July saw me back on my old tug/survey boat *Sprightly*, owned by Korevaar Marine in Melbourne, to conduct a survey for the placing of new telephone cable off Sydney. The job lasted for three weeks and it was nice to have some money coming in for a change as just about all of my savings had been invested in salvage gear, which I hoped would pay for itself one day.

As soon as the survey was complete and the vessel redelivered to Geelong, John Korevaar asked me to go across to Fremantle to take over their grab/hopper dredger *Fremantle*. She was in dock undergoing repairs being readied for a dredging contract in Dampier up on the North West coast. After about a fortnight we were all ready to sail, when word was received that the dredging contract had been delayed so everybody was sent home again to await further developments.

In the meantime I had secured a delivery job, so from Fremantle it was back to Singapore again to pick up the ex-supply boat now fishing vessel *Pride of Eden*. She had been purchased by a group of fishermen in Eden amid great fanfare of how they were going to revolutionise the Australian fishing industry. Having no great faith in some of the principles of the company, I had a word to the shipping master in Fremantle and secured a set of Articles for the voyage, although expressly instructed not to do so.

The vessel was in a nice old mess when I arrived and it was another two weeks before we were ready to sail. I had secured the services of my old mate Fred Buzza to come along as chief engineer, which turned out to be a good thing, or else we may never have made the distance. One morning the boss informed us we had to take on bunkers and both Fred and myself told him that we did not know how to take bunkers. The boss was furious and ranted and raved about us being a pair of incompetent buggers. Finally we said that we would take on the fuel, but pointed out that it may take a bit longer than expected, as during the refit all the bunker connections had been cut off at deck level and the steel plates welded over! The whole of the refit had been carried out the same way. The only interest had been the fishing gear, nobody had ever looked at the machinery, inside tanks or the ship's original piping system.

While in Singapore I took the opportunity to look up some old acquaintances with a view to future work prospects and on September 30th, we finally sailed for Eden. The trip down south definitely proved that apart from the fishing gear, nothing else had been looked at during her rebuild in Singapore. The gyro compass was the first to go and so much fishing electronics had been placed in the wheelhouse, the magnetic compass was next to useless. One generator was out with a cracked head, the purifier worked only sometimes, the refrigeration stuffed up and I was unable to get the main radio working. Luckily, the weather was good for most of the passage and we anchored in Twofold Bay early in the morning of October 20th. Our four and a half thousand mile passage had taken 19 days, averaging just under ten knots.

Two days after arrival the owners arranged a grand party with all the town heroes and various politicians attending; of course we were not invited. Problems immediately arose over wages and repatriation expenses and the bosses wanted us out of sight and well clear of the ship before the arrival of the VIPs. It was then I produced the ship's Articles, all signed and officially stamped. I at once became the most unpopular man in Eden. All monies owing were paid and air tickets given to the crew members who lived in Singapore. Even today I do not think that I have been totally forgiven.

1987 ended with two small salvage jobs, a fishing boat forty miles to the south of Eden and a power boat lifted from the bottom of a lake in the Snowy Mountains. All in all it had not been a bad year, a variety of work and the bank balance still in the black. The New Year brought a lot of activity with a number of inquiries coming in for local work and a number of offers from overseas. Some of the inquiries were genuine but quite a number were rather dodgy and I ended up joining the dredger *Fremantle* in Dampier, WA. The *Fremantle* was an old clanger dating from 1954, she was a small grab hopper dredger of 345 gross tons, but she was a handy little ship for certain jobs.

There had been a very big dredging programme in Dampier and now all that remained were high spots left by the cutter suction dredger. They had to be drilled and blasted and then the debris collected by grab. It was loaded aboard the *Fremantle* then dumped in the spoil ground. She was working 24 hours with two crews on 12 hour shifts. We were living ashore, so from leaving the pub until arriving back after shift totalled a 14 hour working day. We had real good crews who were happy in the job and never complained.

The French dredging contractors appreciated our attitude and looked after us well. They told us some real horror stories of the continuous union problems that they had experienced during the main dredging phase. The money was good, the beer at the pub even better and every week we received a cash bonus for our efforts. Within six weeks the job was all over, the ship was cleaned down and laid up in Dampier at a cyclone mooring. That was my first dredging operation and although life was rough and ready, I really enjoyed the work, even though it could be fairly repetitive. We had a character aboard who was known throughout the industry as "Freddie Dredge", he kept telling me how hard the job was and it was certainly a lot easier when he went home on leave.

I flew back to Melbourne to have a meeting with John Korevaar. He had a sale for the old *Sprightly* and now wanted to get back into the coastal towing business. He had his eye on a tug from Adelaide, the *Eureka II* and the decision was made to purchase the vessel and that I should go master. Within a week of returning to Eden, a large pleasure cruiser sunk at her moorings in Twofold Bay. The new salvage equipment was mobilised and a day later she was raised and safely put on the slipway. At last some return was beginning to show on my investment.

Picking up my old mate Vic Krisenthal as chief, we flew to Adelaide to slip the *Eureka II* and get her ready for coastal towing work. She was not a bad little tug, only 220 gross tons, 32 metres in length and a 20 ton bollard pull. She was fairly well equipped but basically only a harbour tug and with her hydroconic hull, turned out to be a far from good sea boat, very uncomfortable and very wet in any bad weather.

In Adelaide the tug was slipped and put through survey, fuel and stores were loaded and Korevaar's regular crew were flown over for the voyage to Geelong. It was then that the trouble started with the maritime unions. We had 14 bunks aboard the tug and the demand was for 14 crew — all on film star wages — to sail on the delivery voyage. Unfortunately, these union problems persisted the entire time that the vessel operated on coastal towing, eventually forcing the tug to be sold overseas and men being put out of work. When there are no more ships left in the Australian fleet, these same unionists will sit back and wonder what went wrong.

We finally sailed from Adelaide on a very rough passage to Geelong and I knew that there was a lot more work to do on the ship. Among other things, you practically needed oilskins to keep watch in the wheelhouse, and every hatch, port and watertight door leaked like a sieve. In Geelong we took delivery of new towing gear and arranged for the fitting of a gyro compass, autopilot and satellite navigator. New seals were fitted to watertight doors and portholes.

On May 14th 1986 we departed Geelong with our first tow: two barges bound for Brisbane. We had a crew of ten men aboard, enough to work three watches and to handle the two sets of towing gear when streaming or recovering. The *Eureka II* had no towing winch, so the two sets of tow gear were attached to either side of the

Recovering towing gear on the Eureka II

main tow bollard which had been beefed up and enlarged to enable the heavy wires to be turned up. The large tow *Leyton Candec 1* was towed on a combination of synthetic towline and wire with a total length of 530 metres, whilst the smaller tow *LC 3* was on slightly lighter gear at a variable length of about 400 metres.

The voyage to Brisbane was not without its problems, the weather off the east coast was far from perfect and we experienced a lot of electrical problems. The 1,100 mile voyage occupied ten and a half days at an average speed of 4.6 knots, and both tows were safely delivered. The tug was redelivered back to Geelong, where further work was put in hand on the tug and Vic and myself headed back to Eden.

In Eden, there was a bit of drama going on, as the tug *Tasman Hauler* (ex-BP *Cockburn*, built 1959, 419 gross tons) had been left unattended on a mooring and had blown ashore on to the rocky shores of Twofold Bay. I was in Geelong at the time working on the *Eureka II* and drove home through the night to see if I could be of any assistance. Unfortunately I did not hit it off with the new manager of Chartercraft and Marine Services, the local tug company, and my offer to act as salvage master and to provide pumps and patching material were declined. After a few days she was refloated in a severely damaged condition and was uneconomical to repair.

She was sold to a local diver for a nominal sum as was the tug *Henry Bolte* (393 gross tons, built 1966). I assisted him in stripping both vessels and preparing them for scuttling. Some time later I had the pleasure of being the last man aboard to open the main sea injections, prior to both vessels slipping beneath the waves to become artificial reefs for recreational divers. They certainly turned out a great success and a real money booster for the town, as today divers come from all over to 'dive the wrecks' off Twofold Bay.

With the loss of the *Tasman Hauler*, Chartercraft were looking around for a replacement vessel for their coastal towage operations. I tried to talk my pal John Korevaar into buying the *Wongara* (built 1970, 423 gross tons) which was in the hands of a fisherman in South Australia. However, money was short and she ended up the new flagship of the Eden tug fleet, much to my disappointment.

Our next job was at home in Eden, where the airbags were put to good use. A Naval mooring system was recovered from the seabed in Twofold Bay and landed ashore. We did not make much money but hoped that it would be a good foot in the door with the Navy.

In October I received a telephone call from a mate in Singapore who urgently required a skipper for his salvage tug for a couple of weeks. The day after arriving I flew down to Bengkulu on the southwest coast of Sumatra to pick up the tug *Sai Hong* (built 1967, 350 gross tons, 38 ton bollard pull). She was a nice little tug, but in a hell of a mess, originally built in France and with a Thai crew.

Our tow was the cutter suction dredger *Vlaanderen XI* and the sheer legs barge *Gajah I* to Port Kelang in the Malacca Strait. Luckily the tug was on continual hire as it was three weeks before the dredger was ready to sail. The time was spent cleaning the tug up and over-hauling the towing gear, which was sadly neglected. There was a lot of trouble with the towing winch throughout the passage which meant a prolonged stop over-anchored off Singapore carrying out repair work. We finally delivered our two charges alongside at their destination in Malaysia after a rather slow trip, averaging only just over three knots for the 1,300 mile tow. The tug was returned to Singapore and after eight weeks away I paid off and flew back home to Eden, it had been an experience and I have never eaten Thai food again.

At the end of 1988 I made contact with David Roberts of Sunderland Marine Insurance and commenced survey work on their behalf. An excellent working relationship built up between us and even today I still do work for them on an occasional basis on surveys, salvage, towage approval and legal cases.

Early in the New Year it was back down to Geelong again to prepare the *Eureka II* for her next offshore contract. That time we had two dumb hopper barges to tow from Melbourne to Brisbane. They were two ex-Port of Melbourne heavy older style units and they towed very well. We averaged well over five knots for the

1,160 mile passage. By that stage the *Eureka II* was very well equipped with Hiab crane, Zodiac inflatable, good tow gear and electronics, and a rebuilt wheelhouse with no leaks. We had a really good crew who knew the boat and we all hoped for a lot more work in the future.

After arriving back at our base in Geelong it was home to Eden for a week and then back down south for the next job. The *Eureka II* had been hired to assist in the construction of an ocean outfall at Seaspray on Victoria's ninety mile beach. Our tow was the Geelong crane barge *Robert Purnell*, and to assist in the operation Korevaar's smaller tug *Stockton* accompanied us. We had several days of weather delays prior to sailing and when we did finally get underway we arrived at the Heads at the wrong time: the start of the flood tide. As a result we were stuck in the Rip for about four hours, making no headway and just holding our own against the incoming tide. The tide finally turned and we sailed clear only to be confronted by a southwest gale with a heavy sea and swell. Upon rounding Wilson's Promontory conditions improved and we headed towards the construction site.

The weather was exceptionally bad for the time of year and there was a lot of time lost when it was just too dangerous to work in the surf zone off Seaspray. The outfall pipe was the culmination of a large operation and the contractors were not taking any chances in completing the last stage, as the whole contract could be ruined. Some six weeks passed before the job was completed and the tug and tow returned to Geelong.

The rest of the year was fairly quiet and despite many inquiries nothing eventuated. Money was still going out on more salvage gear so in desperation I telephoned Australian Offshore and was instructed to fly to Singapore to take over one of their vessels to carry out some oilrig tows. Arriving at Changi Airport at midnight, the chief engineer and myself hung around for most of the night and joined the *Lady Florence* (built 1981, 5,750 hp) early in the morning in the Western Anchorage. We had a total of nine crew, the rest were Filipinos and most had never been on a tug before.

No time was wasted and by 1800 hours that evening we were hooked up to the *Maersk Venturer*, a 10,000 ton displacement jack-up oilrig. The mate was hopeless and for the first 24 hours, I was on the bridge working our way through the Singapore Strait at the grand speed of two knots. We were double towing with another supply boat, the *Gabbiano Rossi*, which was a gutless wonder and had great difficulty in keeping station. First stop was at Batam where we waited for seven days for the necessary clearances and a good weather forecast. The rig could only jack down in less than a one-and-a-half metre swell and as it was now increasing northeast monsoon weather, it could turn out to be a long job.

The five day tow to the location averaged only two-and-a-half knots and we were a further four days stooging about until the swell eased off and the rig could be positioned. During the tow I wanted to pay out more wire because of sea conditions, but the other boat had no more wire left on his winch and I knew that I was back in the oil patch world with their super efficiency.

Christmas day saw us steaming back to Singapore after finally getting the rig positioned at midnight. Christmas fare was excellent, the 'cook' was seasick in his bunk, so toasted sandwiches were the order of the day. There was certainly not much sleep for me on that job. The night before arriving back at Singapore, I handed over to the mate at 2200 hours with three hours to run to the Horsburgh Light and tried to grab a couple of hours shut eye. I was back on the bridge at 0100 hours only to find the ship six miles to the south of where we should be and about to run aground.

I had complained to the company about bad vibrations and said that I suspected propeller damage. After much complaining (nobody had complained before) they agreed to put her in dry dock. Needless to say, both propellers were very badly damaged and of course it was all my fault. What a mob they turned out to be. I also contacted the Melbourne office telling them that I was not happy with the job or having to work 24 hours a day since the mate was an idiot. It was definitely not the done thing to complain, however, just read the safety manuals and keep quiet.

We left Singapore in early January towing the jack-up rig *Trident XII* (another 10,000 ton displacement rig), but at least that time there was a decent mate aboard with whom to share the workload. That time we were bound for Brunei. The other towing vessel was the *OSA Alexandersturm*, and luckily the weather was good as she kept falling off course the entire voyage. That meant we had to reduce power and follow her around in order to regain our course.

The 760 mile tow was completed in nine days at an average speed of three-and-a-half knots. As soon as the rig was placed on location it was straight back to Singapore where I paid off after nine weeks. More arguments arose over airline tickets, but I managed to change the flight and spend a few days in town looking up old mates. I booked into my usual hotel and received a message that had arrived from Australia the day I had left the ship. I telephoned David Roberts at Sunderland Marine and received instructions to meet him in Melbourne on my arrival. Arriving at Melbourne at 2200 hours, I checked into a hotel for a few hours sleep and at seven the following morning, I was on the plane to Adelaide.

The large fishing vessel *Karina G* had grounded off Eucla in the Great Australian Bight, so from Adelaide we chartered a plane and flew to Eucla for an inspection. She was well aground in the surf zone, practically flooded throughout her length and beginning to fill with sand. On the long trip back with the owner and underwriter, various salvage options were discussed. My idea was that the most cost effective and fastest option (despite mobilisation time) was to get a fully equipped shallow draft salvage tug on site. I contacted my old pal Rainer Kasel in

Singapore and a tender was proposed on that basis. I hoped that by refloating the vessel she could eventually be returned to service, or at least there would be some salved value left over for the underwriters, should they declare a constructive total loss.

However, a firm of ex-service personnel ended up with the contract, their first and last salvage operation. The vessel landed on the beach, in pieces, many months later. Unfortunately this type of thing still goes on, with owners or insurers accepting the cheapest quote, the salvors not knowing what they are doing and the job ends up costing far more than the quotation submitted by a reputable firm.

The months went by and in desperation I started to look for anything that would pay the bills. Result was that I joined the *Iron Sturt*, a 22,000 ton bulk carrier in Newcastle as third mate. This was a bitter pill to swallow after being skipper for so many years, but it was financial necessity and I never intended to make a career out of it. After seven weeks of wandering around the coast carrying a variety of bulk cargoes, the novelty wore off. The bank balance looked a bit healthier and I swore never again to set foot on a big ship unless in the capacity of salvage master, and it was back home to Eden.

Within two days of arriving home, I received a telephone call from the underwriters and embarked on my first court case as expert witness. Mountains of paperwork was received from lawyers and it was head down and bum up preparing evidence for the Federal Court case in Melbourne, dealing with an expensive salvage claim. It was a very interesting experience culminating in four days at court. The case was successful on our side, and since that time I have managed to obtain quite an amount of similar work. Sitting at home in the office when one is in the mood, sifting evidence, making counterclaims and getting paid very good money for your efforts, is not a bad way to earn a living. After all, lawyers do it all the time.

The great fishing venture with the *Pride of Eden* that was to revolutionise the industry had fallen flat after less than three years. The ship had been sold to Indonesia and I was asked to redeliver the vessel. I think that I was the only one involved with the 'blue brick' that ever made any money out of her. Despite a lot of mechanical problems, the trip north was a lot more pleasant than the delivery voyage from Singapore. The weather was excellent, the Indonesian crew were a good mob of lads and we averaged nine-and-a-half knots for the 18 day passage to Bali. In Bali we all enjoyed a few days relaxing around the pool, the other Aussies flew home and I made my way up to Singapore to check out the job situation.

I managed to see Mr Kahlenberg and we enjoyed a nice lunch together. He was looking very old and frail, but it was nice to see the old gent and I knew that he would not be around for too much longer. After a week later I was back on the big iron bird and home to Eden.

Towards the end of November 1990 an unusual little delivery job came up. Another old friend Peter Mounsey was well into the delivery work and he invited me to join him on the river boat *Murray Explorer*, which was lying at Mannum in the Murray River. The boat was like a block of flats on a barge with a very, very shallow draft and very little power. Our first excitement was crossing the bar at the Murray mouth and then she started rolling. Being in the river for all her life, nothing was fixed or lashed down and the first day and night was spent lashing down galley stoves, large refrigerators and everything else aboard. We were lucky with the weather and with calls at Portland and Eden to take on fuel, we anchored in the Hawkesbury River six-and-a-half days after leaving Mannum.

A few days later it was off on another delivery job but that time the ship was a little larger. On December 10th I flew out of Sydney bound for Panama City. The *Combi Star* was a 165,000 deadweight OBO Carrier that was lying off the port bound for the scrap yard in Karachi. She had grounded at Huasco in Chile and ripped most of her bottom out from forward over a length of some fifty metres and was floating on her tank tops. She had limped as far as Panama with dodgy boilers, which were now undergoing repairs. The previous skipper had resigned and I had come to take over. She was just about the biggest ship that I had ever seen, let alone taken charge of. We had a Thai crew and British Officers aboard, who were none too confident that we would make the distance. The main thing was to get started, however.

My first job was to rig large flashing warning lights in the forward holds, the same as we rigged aboard unmanned tows. The idea was that if they started flashing, seawater had completed the electrical circuit and the holds had begun to flood. The man on watch was to immediately stop the engines and sound the general alarm, that way we would have a chance to abandon ship before she went to Davey Jones Locker.

Ten days later we sailed and getting away from the crowded anchorage was quite a feat in itself, as we were only operating on about 50% power and she was certainly a bit different to handle than a tug. Two hours later we had our first stoppage and drifted all night before getting underway again at noon at the grand speed of eight knots. After getting another thirty miles across the Pacific, we stopped again and drifted for another 24 hours as the engineers battled away down below with faulty boilers. After a few more stops and starts it was decided to return to Panama, and a week after leaving we were back in our old anchorage just in time for Christmas Day.

The British Officers had just about had enough and wanted off, our agent was not getting paid and our satellite communications had been cut off due to non-payment of bills; things were not looking good. Work continued for a couple more weeks and once again we attempted to sail, but that time did not even manage to get out of port limits. By that time the Poms threw in the towel and demanded to be sent home. I volunteered to remain, mainly to give some confidence to the Thai crew whom I felt very sorry for. After six weeks, the owners obtained the services of a full Russian crew and so ended my career in the *Combi Star*. It was disappointing that we never finished the job, however the experience of driving a big ship instead of having one hanging off the end of a towline had been good. It was several months later when she did arrive in Taiwan under her own power — those Russian engineers must have been good.

Chapter 10
Qualified: Protection and Indemnity Surveyor

At the beginning of 1991 while back in Australia, small jobs luckily kept the bank balance in the black as it was to be quite some time before another major salvage came along. The salvage equipment had a good work out with the refloating of a small trawler off Bermagui and general survey work was beginning to pick up. The local shipyard had done some conversion work on a barge for Esso Petroleum and for days I had all the pumps in action, carrying out tank testing. Further work for the shipyard consisted of slinging airbags under trawlers to try and reduce their draft to cross the entrance bar into their ship repair facility. That was not the most pleasant of jobs, as the highest tides were always at night. Swimming around in the middle of the night releasing the bags was always a dodgy operation, especially as the area concerned was known locally as 'the shark hole'.

The monotony was finally broken in July when I joined the ex-rig-supply vessel *Derwent Enterprise* in Melbourne to carry out a three week survey contract in Bass Strait. That was not a bad little number and the job was quite successful. The vessel was one of the Lady boats from Australian Offshore Services that had been converted to a trawler. The fishing venture was never profitable, and after being laid up for some years she was bought by a Queensland firm, converted back to a rig-supply boat and is still going well working in the Far East.

In September a call was received from a legal firm in Sydney. There was a Supreme Court case about to come up regarding a botched up salvage operation and they required an expert witness. I immediately accepted the offer and was once again bombarded with mountains of paperwork. Many hours were spent during a number of months preparing evidence and on several trips up to Sydney, culminating in the Newcastle Supreme Court. Once again we were successful and the QC involved was so impressed, he said that I should take it up as a full time job. If it had been ten years earlier I might have accepted his advice. I remembered from my days in London that there were only a handful of experts that held a Master's certificate as well as legal qualifications who were therefore always in high demand.

In February 1992 we had a major salvage operation right on the doorstep. During a very wild night with a strong easterly gale and continuous heavy rain, the bulk carrier *Daishowa Maru*, anchored in Twofold Bay waiting to berth at the chip mill, dragged her anchor and drove ashore on the hard rocky shore, suffering unknown damage. United Salvage who had obtained the salvage contract took me on board and before the salvage team arrived, I undertook a thorough sounding survey around the casualty. Isolated dangers were marked with buoys and the best direction to refloat the vessel was ascertained.

In the meantime the continuous heavy rain had closed the local airport and cut the main highway, so logistical problems arose in getting men and equipment to the site. Unfortunately the two Eden tugs had no proper deep-sea towing gear and the 4,800 hp salvage tug *Keera* was despatched from Melbourne to conduct the refloating operation. The ship was in ballast condition and her grounded position was exposed to rough seas and a heavy swell where she continued grinding on the rocky ledge causing further bottom damage. The authorities had mobilised a large amount of anti-pollution equipment on site as the ship carried over 900 tons of heavy oil and diesel fuel. With the pristine condition of Twofold Bay at risk, authorities were taking no chances should an oil spill occur during the salvage effort. The incident created a large amount of media attention so the salvors could not afford to make any mistakes, with the whole thing being broadcast to every living room in the country.

The *Keera* was made fast on the morning of February 13th and the controlled de-ballasting of the casualty commenced. The weather was fine and at 1015 hours she was gently slid from the rocks and taken to anchor. A full diving and video inspection of her hull revealed massive bottom damage and it was soon realised that the vessel would have to be towed to the repair yard in Japan. The vessel was of 60,000 deadweight tons and had only been constructed in 1986, so even with the substantial damage the ship was still a very valuable asset.

The tug *Austral Salvor* (480 gross tons, built 1986) was sent down from Brisbane to commence the tow, arriving in Eden on February 17th. The tug and tow departed that evening with the casualty passed over to the Japanese tug *Seiha Maru No. 2* (987 gross tons, 8,200 bhp) on February 28th for onward towage to Japan.

The ship was repaired and returned to service and once again became a regular visitor to Eden to load wood chips.

At the beginning of March the trawler *Otama* went ashore near Mallacoota in Victoria. She was insured by a company that shall remain nameless. However, I am pleased to say that they are no longer in business. The vessel's owner approached me for assistance and for three days we tried to get some sense out of the insurance surveyor who had arrived in town, to begin operations. In the end the owner decided to go ahead without approval, but needless to say that the three-day delay lost us the weather window of good conditions. We mobilised all salvage gear to Mallacoota and hired a helicopter to fly men and equipment to the casualty, as she was completely unapproachable by road. Unfortunately the weather beat us and the trawler's bones still lie on the wild and inaccessible beach. The only good thing to come out of that operation was that the owner was paid out and the insurance company finally paid us for our salvage efforts. Whatever the size of the vessel, quick decisions are vital to any successful salvage operation.

That year also saw the end of the tug *Euraka II* on the Australian coast. Unrealistic union demands ensured the demise of still another source of employment. Before she left for Iran I carried out her last tow, a link-span barge from Melbourne to Port Botany. After that tow was completed, the tug was laid up in Eden for some much-needed repair work. A few weeks later she left on a charter to Tidewater to work as a stand-by vessel in Bass Strait, and when that was completed I went down to Welshpool to redeliver her to Melbourne.

That Christmas the old floating crane *Titan* out of Sydney capsized under tow just north of Newcastle, while I headed south from Eden in a local trawler to pick up one of the casualties from the Sydney-Hobart yacht race.

All was quiet until February when I received an urgent call to get across to New Zealand. The Korean fishing trawler *Oyang No. 5* was on fire, abandoned and drifting in the Southern Ocean. A local firm had been granted the contract and they required me as salvage master. Flying across to Christchurch I arrived just after midnight, hired a car at the airport and drove through the night down to Dunedin. After grabbing a couple of hours sleep, the day was spent gathering an assortment of towing gear and fire fighting/de-watering pumps. The tug *Southern Alpha* arrived from Wellington during the afternoon. She was not exactly the type of vessel to go charging off down to the Southern Ocean, being only 26 metres in length.

We sailed south at eight that evening and arrived in the search area late the following night. The crew of the casualty, who had been rescued from the vessel, had reported that the trawl gear had been cut away, all watertight doors closed and one generator left running before they abandoned ship.

The weather was on our side with good visibility but a heavy ocean swell rolling in from the southwest made life aboard our small tug very uncomfortable as we headed some 200 miles south of Dunedin to begin our search. After three days nothing had been sighted despite an aerial search being conducted at the same time. The vessel's underwriters decided to abandon the operation. The tug returned to Wellington and I flew home, the whole exercise had proved to be a bit of a non-event but the pay was good.

A week after returning to Eden, I was asked to fly to Singapore to pick up a supply vessel for New Guinea. That was another disaster job that was doomed to fail from the outset. The vessel was the *Laut Barat*, a real heap of junk that had been hurriedly fitted out with a four point mooring system and nothing else aboard even being checked. Needless to say we had to sail immediately from Singapore and the trip down to Port Moresby was plagued with mechanical problems. I informed the company of our troubles and told them straight out, that whoever designed their new mooring system was an idiot and that it was never going to work. Like anything to do with the oil patch, to tell the company that they are wrong is not the done thing. On arrival at Port Moresby, I was informed that my services were no longer required. I was not sorry to leave however, the vessel was a lemon, and I believe that very shortly after that she was put off hire and returned to Singapore.

In May 1993, I flew down to Melbourne for an interview with the Melbourne Harbour Trust. They were looking for a skipper on their trailer dredge. Being a man of vast dredging experience (from my short stint on the old *Fremantle*) I convinced them that I was the right man for the job. Although this only turned out to be a part-time operation, the dredger provided me with a steady income over the next four years and with good experience. Only when she was sold out of the country, did my dredging days finally come to an end.

The *AM Vella* was built in Newcastle in 1973. She was a twin screw trailing suction hopper dredger of 96 metres in length and having a hopper capacity of 3,000 cubic metres. When I joined her she was engaged in a dredging contract in Taiwan, a long way from her home port of Melbourne and was operating with Australian Officers and Indonesian crew. Flying via Hong Kong I joined her off the southern port of Kaohsiung where she was engaged in the channel dredging of the Naval base just to the north of that port city. As I was a newcomer to that type of dredging, Captain Ricky Richardson remained aboard for the first month teaching me the ropes.

We were not without our problems. The coast of Taiwan supports a huge local fishing industry and during our runs to and from the dumping ground, we were forever running through fishing nets. These were often picked up by the propellers and played havoc with the stern shaft seals, and twice we had to go into dry dock to have them replaced.

We did not complain however as that meant a few days in port and a chance to get ashore. We had our favourite bars and got along real well with the locals.

The Seaman's Mission served cheap beer and the roadside stalls served excellent seafood. The dredger had been in Taiwan for quite some time and was nearing the end of her contract. After completing the work at the Naval base we shifted north along the coast to the port of Tai Chung. Luckily dredging was fairly straightforward as we had started to suffer more and more mechanical problems. The bow thrust unit was the first to go, then main engine gearbox troubles arose and we had further problems with the dredge pump.

The Naval base was interesting work. We suffered a lot of down time having to completely clear the channel for all Naval movements, but it was this passing traffic that added the interest. The year was 1993 but many of the Naval vessels were Second World War vintage including ex-American Destroyers that were fifty years old. They appeared to be in very good condition and equipped with the latest missile systems. I was particularly interested in their salvage craft, American WW2 vessels, a mixture of BAR Class salvage vessels and BAT Class rescue tugs (same as the old *Sprightly*).

There was some strange wording in our contract, something along the lines that when the pilot left the vessel upon leaving Tai Chung, our contract was completed. We completed the work in Tai Chung and were verbally dismissed to sail for Koahsiung, where we were to take on bunkers and stores for the return voyage to Australia. All the time working in Tai Chung, apart from our initial arrival, we had not seen a harbour pilot, so I obtained radio clearance from harbour control and headed south down the Taiwan Strait bound for Koahsiung. About twelve hours after sailing, I received orders to return to Tai Chung. Duly we returned as instructed and entered the port, a pilot came aboard and we immediately sailed again with the pilot to guide us out through the harbour entrance.

Somebody must have read the dismissal clause in the contract, for as soon as the pilot was dropped we proceeded to Kaohsiung with no further problems. Actually during our stay at various ports in the country, I was pleasantly surprised with the Officialdom. We were treated very well with a minimum of fuss and allowed to get on with the job. In Koahsiung the Indonesian crew were paid off and the Australian crew arrived aboard for the delivery run home. As there was a possibility of obtaining further work in Western Australia, we were ordered to proceed to Fremantle instead of her home port of Melbourne. Good weather was enjoyed on the run back to Australia and we arrived back in Fremantle in August 1993.

Upon boarding, the pilot asked if we required a tug to assist in berthing. I told him that we had no bow thruster and although we were twin screw, I could not guarantee the port gearbox. Luckily he ordered a tug to assist for on the first astern engine movement, our port side propulsion died and required major repairs before the old girl was ready for work again.

Once again I was looking for a job. Although the *Vella* had a permanent full time crew, dredging or not, I was only ever employed on a casual basis whenever she was operational. After six weeks at home I received a call from Taiwan. It was a bit of an unusual request from my old mate K T Lu, who ran Asian Salvage Company out of Koahsiung. He was running three large deep sea tugs manned by Filipino crews and he required somebody to bring the vessels up to scratch with towing and salvage equipment, so that they would be capable of tackling any emergency operations in which they may become involved.

So in little over two months after leaving, I was on the plane again heading back to Taiwan. The following three months were not the easiest I have known. Conditions were far from good and the tucker was barely edible but by the time I left, the fleet were well equipped and in a far better state than when I first laid eyes on them. The two older vessels were in a fairly poor state both with general housekeeping and salvage equipment. I set myself up aboard the *Salvage Queen*, a large ex-Japanese tug of 7,500 hp and started work. The *Salvage King*, ex-Australian rig-supply tug of 4,500 hp was also in port and a lot of time was spent aboard her. The other vessel in the fleet was the *Salvage Giant*, another ex-Japanese tug of 10,000 hp, but she was in a lot better state having just been delivered from Japan for her new owners.

The following twelve weeks were spent working aboard all three vessels. I am of the very strong opinion that no matter how many vessels are owned by any particular company, that they should be capable of working together. As such, all salvage and towing equipment should be interchangeable between the various units of the fleet. With that in mind all salvage pump fittings, hoses and air connections were standardised, and if a 100 ton shackle was painted red on one tug, they were also painted red on the other two. It was quite an assignment but after many hours of hard work, my goal was achieved. I like to think that the success enjoyed by Asian Salvage since that time had not a little to do with my efforts.

During my time in Koahsiung there were a couple of diversions. I took the *Salvage Queen* away to escort the Maltese bulk carrier *Victor* into port and prepared a salvage plan to remove a wreck from a reef in American Samoa, unfortunately our bid was unsuccessful. My work completed, it was back home once again just in time to enjoy the Christmas Season in Eden. After three months of a fish and rice diet, the thought of a proper Christmas dinner was practically beyond my comprehension.

Early in the New Year I received a call from the Port of Melbourne asking me to take over the dredger *AM Vella* again, which was back at work in Melbourne. Unfortunately just days before I was due to join, she collided with the *Seaway Mersey* in the South Channel of Port Phillip Bay, which necessitated several weeks of repairs. It was not until the end of February that I was back with my old command once again, but that time I was sailing as mate for the run across to Bunbury, Western Australia, where she had obtained a dredging contract.

Here I must mention that only the cook and myself had been picked up for the job as the remainder of the crew were permanent. Although she had done very little work since I'd left her some six months previously, they were still permanently employed. One could tell that you were working for the Victorian Government, as no private firm could ever have afforded to operate in this manner.

We averaged ten-and-a-half knots for the voyage across the Bight and after a couple of days getting the old girl ready to commence work, I flew home again and left Captain Richardson to the dredging. Two weeks later and it was back to Bunbury for a month where I took over command of the *AM Vella* and continued the dredging programme. Once again we had our fair share of problems. The old girl was beginning to show her age and was beset by mechanical problems, which resulted in quite an amount of down time. The situation was not helped by the contractor's man on site, who complained bitterly at every breakdown. However, work continued despite the problems and steady progress was maintained.

I was not sorry when my month was up and my relief arrived. After a quick hand over it was back home again, where another problem had arisen right on the doorstep that was much more to my liking. The tug *Provincial Trader* of 419 gross tons had sunk in Twofold Bay. She lay upright in quite deep water in the open roadstead and had to be removed, as the sunken wreck presented a hazard to the trawlers and to commercial shipping anchored off the port.

The removal of the wreck was quite beyond my capabilities as far as equipment went, so I approached my old mate Rainer Kasel in Singapore with whom I had kept in close contact for a number of years. Rainer ran a very successful firm called Salvindo Salvage and had built up an excellent reputation in the salvage and wreck removal field. Together we worked out a plan to lift and dispose of the wreck and duly sent off a lump sum quotation to the underwriters. The fact that the vessel belonged to a two-dollar company and was uninsured made things a little more complicated. However in the end, the underwriters covering the Maritime Services Board (who managed the Port of Eden) picked up the tab.

It was a further three months before the contract was finalised. Our quote was 'far too high' according to the powers that be and the job was awarded to a Western Australian diving firm, who had little or no salvage expertise but came up with the right price.

Our plan had included the use of a Salvindo Salvage ship and a sheer legs barge, which would have been mobilised from Singapore. That way the job would have been completed in a reasonable time with certain results. As it turned out it was another two and a half months before work began and it took the successful tenders a further four months to complete the operation. What they ended up getting paid I do not know, but their overall cost would have been well in excess of our original quotation. As far as I know that was the first and last salvage operation that firm ever carried out, as two years later they had completely disappeared from the scene. I guess that the loss incurred on that operation was the final nail in their coffin. Many years later both my own company and that of Rainer Kasel are still going strong. Some underwriters continue to make the same mistakes, however, ignoring the track records of those who actually know what they are doing and take more notice of smooth talkers who promise the earth.

While all this was going on I found time to take Roslyn on a holiday to the Cook Islands and very shortly afterwards my bachelor days were finally over. We pooled our resources and purchased a new home in Eden where we are still happily ensconced. The ground floor is occupied by the office of K Salvage Company, where I have managed to earn a fairly good living ever since.

Towards the end of 1994 another six weeks were spent aboard the *AM Vella* as skipper carrying out dredging operations in Port Phillip and Westernport Bays. It was an easy job and the money was good. I was not over keen on the boring nature of the work, but the ship-handling side of the job kept me sane. The worst part of the dredging was some members of our crew; they were all permanent employees and most of them had been there far too long. As a result they had lost all touch with reality and petty complaints were never-ending. One day when returning to our base in Williamstown, I called up harbour control for permission to enter the river. In doing so I asked over the radio if it was ok for the SW *Vella* to enter. Harbour control queried the name of the vessel, and I explained that SW stood for 'sheltered workshop'. Needless to say that did not go down too well with management.

At the beginning of 1995 I secured a delivery run from Singapore to Brisbane aboard the world's largest dredger, the newly built *Pearl River* of 25,000 ton capacity. Having sailed as master on the smaller *Vella* for quite some time, I thought that the run job may lead to some permanent work. Unfortunately, I was not in the club and an invitation to participate in her Australian dredging programme was not forthcoming.

With my newfound domestic situation there was not much incentive to go charging off overseas again and I was quite content to sit at home and to try to make a living out of survey work. The work had picked up and I was covering most of the fishing fleet from Ulladulla to Lakes Entrance. Although not making a fortune, at least the bills were being paid and I was home just about every night.

In June, one of the small gas tankers arrived in Eden to take on fuel. The mate had gone off sick and they were after somebody to sail with her to Westernport. The local agent introduced me to the skipper, a Kiwi by the name of Rob Mitchell, and I'm pleased to say we hit it off immediately. The following day we sailed for Westernport and that was to be the start of an extended involvement with Boral Gas. In July 1995 I joined the *Boral Gas*, a small LPG Carrier of 2,062 gross tons. We loaded a full cargo in Westernport and proceeded on a voyage around the Pacific Islands to discharge. My position aboard was as extra mate, with the idea that once I had mastered the world of gas carriers I would sail as relieving master on an occasional basis when required to do so.

As both the tankers belonging to the company were regular callers at Eden, this seemed like a good opportunity to pick up some casual work and not be away too long from home. The first trip with Rob Mitchell was very interesting and he was more than willing to pass on his knowledge about a trade that I knew virtually nothing about.

After leaving the Australian coast we called at Nukualofa, Pago Pago, Labasa, Lautoka, Eden and then back to Westernport. We had a Tongan crew aboard and they were a good mob of blokes to work with, hard workers and always had a smile on their faces, which was a pleasant change from the inmates in the 'sheltered workshop'. Apart from the carriage of liquid petroleum gas there was a lot to learn, including pilotage through the reef-strewn waters of the South Pacific. Passage through the waters to the north of Suva was different to say the least, winding our way through many miles of reefs marked only with the occasional bamboo pole with a rusty tin can as a topmark. Securing to dilapidated moorings at the various ports, stenching the cargo and carefully calculating the correct amount of gas pumped ashore, all lead to a very interesting and rewarding trip. The round trip took about five weeks, and I managed to get in two voyages that year.

On the second voyage we loaded in Indonesia and after doing the rounds of the islands I flew home from Honiara, not realising that I would return here under very different circumstances in five years time. The company also sent me down to Melbourne to complete a Gas Tanker Safety Course.

Unfortunately early in 1996 the manning contract for the two gas tankers was taken over by BHP. They had their own personnel and did not require the services of a relieving skipper, so my short career came to an end. However 1996 was the year that I finally got back into the salvage game and apart from a few run jobs, have been engaged in this capacity ever since. Before completely severing all ties with *Boral Gas*, I was commissioned to give a report and provide recommendations regarding all their mooring systems around the Pacific. Heaven knows they certainly needed a lot of improvement, but I don't know if any action was taken on my recommendations.

The year started off well and much time was spent at home working on a court case for the Victorian Solicitor General. Preparations went on for months and once again it was a case of head down and bum up, buried under that mountain of paperwork trying to sort out evidence that had been presented at a hearing many years before. The case was finally settled towards the end of the year; there was no court appearance and the whole exercise was very successful for both the State of Victoria and myself.

As the preparation for the court case did not occupy full time work, February found me once again back on the dredger working in Melbourne. When I arrived she was in a hell of a mess, despite being laid up for over a year with a full crew employed. We suffered a number of mechanical problems before commencing operations, which together with never-ending crew trouble, made life aboard none to pleasant during the six-week preparation period. The management gave very little support and the regular employees continued to get away with murder. If it had been a private dredging company, I would say about 90% of them would be unemployed. Despite the good money and the excellent working conditions, the crew mentality was 'take what you can and give nothing in return'. When the dredger was sold overseas the following year, there were a lot of very long faces with the usual grumbles about putting Australian seamen out of work. It was definitely a retrograde step on the part of the Port Authority to dispose of their dredging capability, but I had no sympathy with those who had helped bring about their own demise.

An article appeared in the Lloyds List newspaper regarding a new firm of Protection and Indemnity Correspondents being formed in Sydney. As the P & I Clubs are heavily involved in the world of wreck clearance and oil pollution from marine casualties, I arranged for an appointment with the Principal in Sydney. As a result I became a Commercial Correspondent in the Port of Eden for various members of the international group. Not knowing too much about protection and indemnity insurance, one of the prerequisites of obtaining the position was to undertake a distance learning course in the subject. The course was a quasi-legal one and at fifty-six years of age, my tired old brain cells struggled along for eighteen months studying the textbooks and completing numerous written assignments, which were sent back to England for appraisal. In the end my efforts paid off and adorning my office wall is a Certificate of P & I Insurance, marked 'achieving a pass with distinction'. Long before completing the course however, I was thrown in at the deep end and attended my first casualty in the role of Protection and Indemnity Surveyor.

The *Peacock* was a Panamanian reefer ship of 6541 deadweight tons. While on a ballast voyage from Singapore to New Plymouth, New Zealand, she grounded on Piper Reef which is located just to the south of Torres Strait in the Great Barrier Reef. United Salvage were contracted to salvage the ship under Lloyds Open Form and I was appointed by the Japan P & I Club, through Aus Ship P & I, to attend the salvage operation and look after their interests. The actual salvage costs would be paid for by the vessel's hull underwriters, while pollution prevention and damage to the reef would be covered by the Protection and Indemnity Club.

The area of the stranding some 320 miles to the north of Cairns was very isolated and it took a bit of organising to reach the casualty. I took a commercial flight from Merimbula to Sydney, then on to Cairns, then a charter flight from Cairns to the Lockhart River airstrip and was then airlifted to the casualty on the Salvor's helicopter, arriving on site five days after the vessel had gone up on the reef.

This delay in being appointed made it a bit awkward as a lot of things had been happening and I had a lot of catching up to do. Fortunately I knew the boys from United Salvage and our relationship was very open with no withholding of information. They kept me fully informed of their salvage plan and daily progress reports. Not so easy was dealing with all the other parties involved, and trying to keep track of personnel and equipment on site. With a vessel aground on the Great Barrier Reef, there seemed to be a cast of thousands involved and what should have been a straightforward refloating operation was blown out of all proportion.

Peacock *on* Piper Reef, Pacific Salvor *standing by*

Paranoia reigned supreme, with most of those involved unable to see the wood for the trees. In other words, the prime objective of removing the stranded vessel from the reef without causing pollution took second stage to the highly unlikely scenario of mermaids being washed ashore covered in heavy black fuel oil. That there were no mermaids present, made little difference to the overall way of thinking. My personal opinion is that the whole incident was turned into a massive anti-pollution exercise, with the P & I Club expected to pick up the bill at the end of the day. Weeks later as I spent days poring over submitted accounts from Government and quasi-Government departments, I do not think that I was far off the mark and the red pencil came into very good use.

One stipulation made by the authorities was that the casualty was not to be dragged from the reef, but that it had to be allowed to float free. That in itself was a ridiculous statement; a vessel grounding at a speed of 17 knots would already have caused whatever reef damage had occurred. Dragging it off the reef with a 44 ton bollard pull tug could not possibly damage it further. However the salvors were stuck with the order and had to make their plans accordingly. The fact that the vessel was in light condition with no cargo aboard left few options but to try to transfer fuel oil to improve trim and to further discharge fuel oil to an attendant barge, in order that minimal pull would be required to refloat.

Before discharge of fuel was allowed to commence, all anti-pollution booms and equipment had to be in place and no less than seven chartered vessels, apart from the salvor's own vessels, were on site together with two Marco oil-recovery boats. Even in the near perfect weather conditions experienced throughout the operation, it is doubtful if the equipment on site would have proved suitable if a major spill had occurred, as most of the gear was totally unsuitable for operating in open sea conditions.

In the meantime we were inundated with 'experts' in the fields of sea-grass, dugongs, turtles, crocodiles and sacred Aboriginal sites. That the salvors did not bend over backwards to facilitate all those experts was not very well received. In any salvage situation, the salvors main concern is always to keep the pollutants in the ship, thereby avoiding the need to worry about things that may never happen. While the salvors were getting on with their job, my task was to keep a tab on all the vessels, personnel and equipment that were involved in anti-pollution measures. Being in ten places at once, taking copious notes and myriad photographs, I just hoped that I was gathering sufficient information to compile a reasonable report and to be able to deal with enquiries and accounts that would be coming in long after the whole job was completed.

Three days after my arrival the casualty was towed free of the reef by the tug *Pacific Salvor* (built 1970, 432 gross tons, 44 tons bollard pull), with most fuel oil having being transferred to the landing barge *Pacific Explorer* beforehand.

The casualty was towed clear and safely anchored where the fuel oil was reloaded aboard and she prepared to continue her voyage, a thorough diving and video inspection of the hull revealing no underwater structural damage. However, some latent defects had been found with her steering gear and the authorities insisted on her being towed to Cairns in order to carry out permanent repairs.

After refloating, the area of the grounding had to be carefully examined and photographed to ascertain any damage caused to the reef, to guard against any future claims by the marine park authority. The following day I flew back to Cairns and handed the job over to the local P & I correspondent before heading home to begin writing up reports. Over the few weeks that followed when back in Eden, the accounts started coming in, requiring examination in minute detail. The various authorities must have had a dozen bureaucrats working full time, as not one item was missed. With every item I queried, I had to prepare a carefully written submission.

Going through the bills, I had to keep reminding myself that not one drop of oil was spilt during the salvage operation. So why did bills for cleaning of equipment, spare parts, work wear, seabird rescue kits, camping gear, sun glasses, processing hundreds of photographs, etc have be picked up by the liability insurers? I still have files of paperwork cluttering up the office all well decorated with red pen. I only hope that the hours spent paid off in the end for the club.

That was my first taste of bureaucracy in salvage, but unfortunately it certainly was not my last. Having carried out much more complicated operations in the past, with little or no government interference, it was all just a bit hard to take. However, as more people with little or no practical knowledge become involved in marine operations, things will only become worse. The day will come when the bureaucrats will prevent salvors from getting on with the job and we will have a real ecological disaster on our hands.

After completion of the *Peacock* operation another call was received to proceed to the *Niaga 46*, an 8,000 ton cargo ship aground on Christmas Island. However the job was all over before leaving Sydney, so it was back home again to wait for the next one.

Chapter 11
Kasel Salvage Singapore

Towards the end of August 1996 the Melbourne Harbour Trust was again in touch. Dredging was about to resume again in Melbourne and I was required to commence work at the beginning of September. After all the problems of the last swing, the prospect was not all that attractive, but I swallowed my pride and accepted the position. However, just days before flying down to join the *AM Vella* again, my old pal Rainer Kasel telephoned from Singapore. They had secured a mooring contract in Lhokseumawe, north Sumatra, and desperately required a salvage master to oversee the operation. I made a quick call to the Melbourne Harbour Trust with my humblest apologies and on the night of August 27th, I was on the plane to Singapore.

My previous dealings with Rainer were when we had put in a quote for raising the tug *Provincial Trader* in Eden. Since that date, despite a lot of ups and downs, he was slowly but surely making progress in the world of salvage and wreck removal. From Singapore I boarded a flight for Medan and then a private oil company flight to the port city of Llokseumawe.

The oilrig supply vessel *Swissco* had already left from Singapore with a team of divers and all the equipment that would be needed for the contract. Located off the main oil and gas refinery was an offshore loading facility for tankers. The facility had been sadly neglected over a number of years and our job was to recover the various chain legs of the mooring and secure them to new mooring buoys. The large two-and-three-quarter inch diameter stud link chains were located by towing a large grappling hook across the seabed in the general area, as the plans with which we had been provided were far from reliable.

Once we had snagged something, the winch wire was hauled tight and a diver was sent below to try and ascertain what part of the mooring system was snagged. That was not an easy operation as a deep layer of mud covered the sea floor and we were diving in depths from 160 to 180 feet using only air. A diver's bottom time was limited to about 30 minutes, followed by two hours decompression time which included in-water stops and time in the chamber. The chamber had to be clear before another diver was sent below and we could only have a man on the bottom for a total of two hours in a twelve-hour working day.

Sometimes an entire day would be wasted snagging rubbish on the seabed without recovering a single chain. On other days, strong currents would severely limit the amount of underwater work as we could only put one man on the bottom at a time and after thirty minutes the diver would be physically exhausted. When the end of a mooring chain was recovered and brought on deck, a new mooring buoy was towed out from shore, lashed alongside our work boat and re-secured to the chain. The cylindrical buoys weighed 18 tons and were not the easiest things to handle.

At the end of each working day we remained anchored on site. The Indonesian crew cooked up a feed of fish-heads and rice and we collapsed into our luxurious quarters. This was a shipping container on deck fitted out with six bunks and one mattress on the deck (mine), but at least it was air-conditioned.

All things considered the job went off quite well. The work was successfully completed with no accidents and nobody ended up with 'the bends'. Once the moorings had been completed, the remainder of the job was a visual bottom inspection of the PLEM (pipeline end manifold) and hoses. This was purely a diving operation so the remainder was left in the very capable hands of the chief diver, Jeff Watson, a crazy Yank with whom I have worked with many times since and who proved to be an excellent man to have on any salvage operation.

Leaving the ship I booked into the Lhokseumawe Hilton for the night. Even though it was a bit rough, the beer was cold and the bed more comfortable than the deck aboard the *Swissco*. Unfortunately, the oil company plane to Medan was not operating on account of the thick smoke that was covering the whole of Sumatra from the forest fires.

The following day saw me take an eight-hour taxi ride through the jungle to civilisation. That was by far the most dangerous part of the job and I learnt a few new road rules:

— one must always overtake on blind corners and the crest of hills
— whenever passing through a village or built up area, one must never take one's hand off the horn.

During that long and very remote drive, I tried not to think that a lone European would make a good hostage to members of the Free Aceh Movement who were active in the area. Somehow we arrived in one piece, only to find that the main airport was also closed because of the smoke and it was a further three days before arriving back in Singapore.

The start of 1997 saw me back home again with nothing much in the pipeline. Survey work kept the bank balance ticking over and then in March it was back to Melbourne for the final dredging swing before the old *Vella* was laid up for the last time, prior to being sold. Four weeks were spent working in the River Yarra, daytime shift only and tying up each night at Williamstown. In the evening the crew all went home after work and I had the ship to myself until we commenced again at six the next morning. Things had not improved, Skilled Maritime were about to take over all the floating plant of the Harbour Trust, and the crew who had all been there for years could see the writing on the wall.

That swing we shifted 32,000 tons of spoil from the berths in the river, but after that all channel dredging ceased. Now, some five years later, the port is rapidly silting up. The ships using the port are getting bigger and unless the Port Authority gets their act together very soon, Melbourne will go from being Australia's number one container port to a forgotten backwater devoid of shipping.

In August that year the 19.5 metre wooden trawler *Lochiel* collided with the breakwater and sunk in Ulladulla Harbour on the south coast of New South Wales. The vessel's underwriters, Sunderland Marine, were in immediate contact and I drove up there through the night to survey the vessel and formulate a salvage plan. For the few years previous I had carried out an amount of work with this company and I only wish that there were a few more around like them. After a quick telephone call to their Melbourne manager, I was told to get on with the job. No haggling over costs or how the job should be done, just go ahead and do it and all the paperwork could be figured out later on.

Although the job proved to be very rewarding, both financially and in terms of job satisfaction, the after effects left a bitter taste in my mouth caused by petty officialdom that dragged on for many months after the operation had been completed.

Upon returning to Eden the four salvage crew and myself loaded up three vehicles with salvage equipment from the K Salvage store. Although the casualty was located in the centre of a busy regional town, I was proud of the fact that we went fully prepared and apart from hiring an air compressor on site we were otherwise self-contained. The crew consisted of rigger, shipwright and two divers, all of whom I had worked with before. The gear consisted of airbags, pumps, diving gear, generator, patching material and a full range of miscellaneous tools and equipment that might be needed.

Upon arrival the local authorities had placed an oil boom around the vessel and the local fire brigade were on hand to offer any assistance. The first diving inspection revealed the source of the fuel leakage and ventilator pipes were blocked to prevent further pollution. While all loose debris from the vessel was lifted ashore, the divers measured up the large hole that had been punched in the hull and patching material was prepared.

The following day, ten fully enclosed airlifting bags with a total lift of 32 tons were installed both internally and externally to the hull. Two diesel and six electric submersible pumps were readied to commence de-watering once the deck of the vessel was lifted clear of the water. The underwater damage was patched and the lifting operation began. Despite our best efforts the first attempt was unsuccessful. This was mainly due to the fact that none of the vessel's watertight compartments were actually watertight. My plan had been to first raise the stern of the vessel and then by progressive pumping of compartments, to work from aft to forward until the vessel was safely afloat.

That second night the vessel was allowed to resettle on the harbour bed while we rethought our plans, which included the hiring of a crane which was hooked onto the forward end of the trawler, to keep her stable during the actual lift. The next morning saw an early start and by noon the crane was fast forward and all airbags had been inflated. Pumps were swung into action, but further underwater patching was necessary before they started to take effect and the level of water inside the hull began dropping. The situation was under control by six that evening. The crane was dismissed and the ingress of water was easily handled by a single pump running intermittently.

The salvage crew stood by all night with the casualty safely moored alongside. Patches were checked and all pumps were kept on standby in case anything untoward happened. The following morning the external airbags were removed and the vessel towed across the harbour and placed on the slipway. Our temporary patch was removed, revealing the considerable extent of the underwater damage explaining why she went down so quickly.

The job was not yet over and after loading the salvage gear, three of the boys returned to Eden while Alan Cameron and myself stayed behind to carry out machinery preservation work. In order to minimise loss it is essential that any machinery capable of preservation is tackled as soon as possible, and both the main engine and generator were saved by prompt action thus saving time and money to both owner and underwriters.

From our arrival on site to the vessel being safely on the slip occupied three days and nights of hard work and I was feeling justifiably happy with the result. The operation had created a great deal of media attention but unfortunately the NSW Workcover Inspector was among those to have seen the TV coverage.

The two divers employed were commercial abalone fishermen, who had been diving for years in the open sea off the rugged south coast of New South Wales. That job had them diving in three metres of water inside a sheltered harbour, and, according to the Inspector, that was very dangerous and broke all the rules as they did not possess commercial diving qualifications. I dare say the poor fellow would have had a heart attack if he had been with me on the Lhokseumawe mooring job. However one cannot argue with bureaucrats and their rulebook, so months after I received a rather hefty fine and was told not to do it again.

In November it was back to Singapore with the intention of returning to Lhokseumawe to witness the berthing of the first tanker at the revamped offshore mooring. The plans were very soon delayed, as the night I arrived the worst pollution incident ever to occur in the Singapore Strait took place when two large tankers collided. The following morning I was placed aboard the 140,000 ton tanker *Evoikos*. She had collided with the 268,000 ton tanker *Orapin Global*, and 30,000 tons of heavy fuel oil had spilt from her ruptured tanks.

The salvage contract for the vessel had been obtained by the Greek salvor, Tsavliris International, and I had been appointed acting salvage master by Kasel Salvage. As such it was my job to oversee oil spill response measures, conduct a diving survey of the damaged hull and to commence preparation for the ship-to-ship transfer of her remaining cargo.

She was a big ship and the extent of the damage was hard to comprehend. The bow of the other vessel had sliced half way through the *Evoikos* and she was in a very weakened state. As a result, a very carefully planned discharge sequence would be required if the vessel was not literally to snap in half and the Naval architect burned up the hours on his laptop to ensure that this did not happen. After witnessing the debacle on the Barrier Reef when not one drop of oil was spilt, I was glad that the 'sea grass man' was not peering over my shoulder asking stupid questions.

As soon as I was relieved on the *Evoikos* by a salvage master flown out from Greece, it was a quick trip back to Lhokseumawe and aboard the 48,000 ton tanker *Olga* to berth at the offshore mooring. That time I arrived at Medan late at night and had to find a car to take me on the eight-hour horror trip to the oil port. After a fair amount of haggling we were on our way through the jungle in the dead of night, hoping that I had chosen wisely and would not end up mugged along the way and dumped by the side of the road or taken hostage. We arrived safely but I vowed never to do the trip again unless it was daylight as we had some very close calls, with trucks and buses going full speed down the centre of the road and not giving way for anybody.

Rainer Kasel had instructed me to take plenty of photographs but as my camera was confiscated on arrival, I had to make do with drawing plans, taking bearings from the ship and using a small pocket range-finder. Luckily those plans sufficed as after my report, our contract from the previous August was settled and completed.

After another horrific drive back to Medan, two more days were spent hanging about the hotel waiting for the airport to open as it was closed again due to the smoke from the forest fires. After a day in Singapore to finish off the report, it was home again to Eden.

Within a week of arriving home I received an urgent call from Rainer to get myself to Djakarta immediately: we had landed the contract to salvage the tug *Bosta Kayung 5*. She had been towing a barge off the southeast coast of Sumatra and in the thick smoke haze, had nearly been run down by a passing freighter. The ship had passed between tug and tow, fouling the towline and capsizing the tug, and she was now drifting upside down somewhere near the Karimata Strait.

On arrival at Djakarta I booked into a hotel, contacted the local agent and tried to arrange a flight to Palembang the following morning, which was the nearest large town to the position of the casualty. The airport at Palembang had also been closed because of the smoke which was still blanketing most of Indonesia, but our luck held and we managed to get a flight the following morning.

Tug Karya Mitra, *a home from home*

With no equipment, men or a suitable vessel, I had to get out to the casualty. Firstly I had to find it and then try to prevent it from sinking until the salvage barge arrived from Singapore. With the agent and my pocket full of American Dollars, we went hunting for men and equipment — not the easiest assignment in downtown Palembang. I managed to hire three coast guard divers with scuba gear, Zodiac inflatable, a highly suspect air compressor and a decrepit old wooden tug with a local crew. A couple of bags of rice, some fish, vegetables and many cartons of bottled water and we were ready to embark on our journey into the unknown.

After a ninety-mile trip downriver we reached open water and steamed through the smoke haze looking for our capsized tug. Luck was with me once again as late in the night we came across another tug standing by the upturned *Bosta Kayung 5*. We probably would never have found it otherwise as the only navigation gear aboard was a magnetic compass and a short range VHF radio.

Life aboard was not the best. I slept on the deck of the wheelhouse, ate only fish and rice, had no toilet or shower and only hurricane lamps after the sun went down. Nobody spoke more than three words of English and I felt rather lonely, especially as the sea was flat clam and we were in a little world of our own, enclosed by the heavy smoke haze that reduced visibility to less than fifty metres.

When daylight came that first day on site, our casualty was very low in the water and if the weather came up, she would most certainly spill the little air that was keeping her afloat and plunge to the bottom of the sea, never to be seen again. A general plan of the casualty had been faxed down to me in Djakarta and working with this plus lots of sign language and drawings, I sent the divers to work trying to close all the doors and other openings which were now underwater. Later in the afternoon, air was blown into the capsized hull and she began to lift further out of the water. After some time, an estimated fifty more tons of buoyancy had been blown into the casualty and the danger of her sinking unexpectedly had been averted.

The following morning the divers were sent down again to try and secure any remaining openings. No more openings were secured that day; instead they discovered the bodies of the crew trapped inside the upturned hull. The bodies were recovered and placed in the tug's dinghy tied off the stern (that night aboard was far from pleasant). The Indonesians certainly have a different way of thinking as the divers went back into the wreck and caught some crabs, which they offered me for tea. Knowing what crabs eat I politely declined and was pleased when another tug arrived alongside the next day to take our 'guests' ashore.

Finally the salvage barge *Abex* arrived from Singapore. My old pal Jeff Watson was aboard and after a nice hot shower, we sat down for a yarn over a decent meal and a cold beer. Jeff had brought with him two more salvage divers and all the equipment needed to complete the job. The idea was to seal the vessel completely, fill it full of air and parbuckle or roll her over the right way up, then once afloat to de-water her completely.

The next day Jeff discovered that the coast guard divers were not really salvage divers and nothing underwater had even been closed properly. Still, they tried and I was pleased that they were there to do the nasty work before the arrival of the barge. Two days were spent completely sealing the hull, using heavy plywood patches and hook-bolts and finishing the whole lot with underwater epoxy. Strops were made fast to the deck of the casualty and led right around the hull, the ends of which were made fast to heavy tackles on the deck of the barge. In order to gain a little more rotation, strops were also led around the hull and attached to the towing gear of the tug *Oceanic Star* which had towed the salvage barge down from Singapore.

All available tanks on the casualty were blown with compressed air, then air hoses were connected to blow into the engine room and the accommodation. On the second attempt with the deck tackles heaving and the tug pulling at full power, the casualty rolled over but jammed solid against the bow of the barge with a 65-degree list to starboard.

What to do next? Jeff and I decided to take a gamble. The port side doors were opened up and four suction lines from salvage pumps on deck were thrown in. We hoped that we could get the water out of her fast enough, before something untoward happened and she plunged to the bottom. After an hour's pumping the lower deck edge of the casualty came clear of the water, the ship was stable and the danger had passed. Two hours later, all water had been pumped out and she lay with only a three-degree list. Fuel tanks were opened up and after some fuel transfer she was safe and upright.

The following day was spent cleaning up the casualty and carrying out machinery preservation to the two main engines, gear boxes and auxiliaries, putting into practice what Alan Cameron had taught me on the *Lochiel*. Towing gear was rigged and the *Oceanic Star* towed barge and casualty to the mouth of the river to await clearance to leave Indonesian waters and return to Singapore. That was supposed to have been taken care of by our local agent, whom I had left sitting in the hotel in Palembang ten days before. Despite numerous radio calls, there was no response.

Rainer was most anxious for the job to be completed as the tug and barge were on daily hire and the meter was ticking over. I went ashore in the afternoon to a local fishing village (with a good escort as it was said to be a pirate village), found a telephone that worked and rang Singapore. I was told to get to Palembang, try to find our agent and get the clearance to sail. Back on the barge a local water taxi offered to take me the ninety miles upriver to Palembang. The taxi was a long dugout canoe with a damn great outboard motor on the back and was capable of doing about 25 knots. After a bit of haggling a price was agreed; grabbing my gear, we headed off.

To my dismay we headed straight for the pirate village where about a hundred locals met me on the jetty. The village was about five miles from the barge, so no matter how loud I yelled nobody would ever hear me. After smiling a lot and handing out my remaining stock of cigarettes, things settled down and after an hour the boat driver reappeared with his offsider plus a large car battery and a spotlight. The river was full of logs and hundreds of unlit fishing boats, so I knew he was going to be a careful driver. It was with a sigh of relief that we cast off from the village at sunset and headed upriver. Two fuel stops and four hours later we arrived at Palembang.

I was dropped off at a rickety jetty at a very run down part of town and wandering through dark alleys not knowing where the hell I was, began to worry. Still, my luck held and after about twenty minutes found a main road. A friendly taxi driver appeared and I was soon back at the hotel, where I found the agent having his dinner. After a severe talking to, dinner was forgotten and he hot-footed it to the harbour master's house to chase up a port clearance.

The next morning I waited to see the agent on his way to the barge with the necessary clearance and managed to get a flight to Djakarta. After many hours hanging around the airport, I finally stepped aboard the Ansett flight to Sydney. I had been away only fourteen days but it certainly seemed much longer; although only a small operation tonnage wise, the *Bosta Kayung* had proven to be a rewarding challenge.

Shortly after arriving home, Rainer telephoned regarding a passenger ship that had rolled over and sunk in Borneo. It was to be a major parbuckling operation and a lot of time was spent discussing the various options. Early in 1998 he had finalised the contract but had hired a German salvage master for the job and wanted me to return to Palembang to raise a sunken Indonesian tanker that was lying not far from where my last operation had taken place. My pal Alan Cameron was hired as salvage foreman for the passenger ship operation and he flew up to Singapore in January while I waited at home.

About ten days later I received another phone call. The Palembang job was cancelled and Rainer wanted me on the big operation as assistant salvage master. Arriving in Singapore on February 6th, a hectic four days were spent going through the salvage plan and drawing up the list of equipment required with Rainer and the Naval architect.

The *Leuser* was a 6,041 gross ton passenger ship, built in 1994 in Germany and owned by Pelni Lines in Indonesia. She was one of several sister ships that were engaged in the inter-island trade, carrying over 1,000 passengers in cabin and dormitary accommodation. On November 20th 1997 while transiting the Mahakam

River in thick smoke haze, she collided with the log carrier *Kayu Lapis Lima*. A large hole was punched through the side of the vessel extending over four decks and she consequently rolled over and sunk. She now lay on the muddy river bottom with a list of 80 degress and completely flooded throughout. All 1,200 passengers and crew were safely evacuated; given the massive extent of the damage it was amazing that there was not a heavy death toll. Now some three months later, she was not only flooded with water but many thousands of tons of mud were trapped inside the hull.

She lay in a very isolated location, the nearest large town of Samarinda lying some twenty miles up river and even then only very basic supplies and equipment could be procured locally. All craft and salvage equipment had to be mobilised at Singapore and towed to the site some 1,100 miles away. If anything had been forgotten, we would have had to go without as no salvage equipment was available locally.

The ship had to be uprighted using cantilevers, which had to specially designed both to fit the shape of the ship's hull and to withstand the massive forces that would be placed upon them during the uprighting. Pulling barges, anchor patterns and rigging plans all had to be finalised as all the equipment had to be predesigned before loading onto various barges prior to their departure to the salvage site. Working in conjunction with Indonesian joint partners PT Armandi Pranaupaya of Jakarta, all legal technicalities were taken care of.

On February 5th salvage operations commenced with the arrival of the salvage barge *Swissco Marine 9*, a support tug and members of the salvage team. The latter comprised divers, riggers, boilermakers, tug and barge crews and consisted of three Canadians, three Germans, three Australians and up to 80 Indonesians. All had to be fed and housed on site, presenting a major logistal exercise in itself.

At first glance, things could not have been much worse. The casualty was lying on her port side with an 80 degree list and the damage to the hull measured some eight metres by six metres extending over four decks. The bow of the other vessel had penetrated a good third of the way inboard. There was massive internal damage, and superstructure damage extended upwards for another three decks. The river currents were running at five knots and there was zero underwater visibility. With the salvage barge lashed alongside the *Leuser*, work began. A team of boilermakers worked around the clock, cutting away damaged hull plating, decks, bulkheads, pipework and all internal fittings in way of the collision damage. This material was then off-loaded onto the salvage barge and later transferred ashore to the local scrapyard. When all the steelwork had been cut away from the damaged area, complete internal decks, beams, bulkheads and stringers had to be rebuilt in place to get some strength back into the vessel before patching could commence.

Meanwhile the pulling barge *Sea Warrior* had arrived from Singapore under tow, loaded down with salvage equipment, heavy anchors, tackle blocks and fabrication material to construct the main patch, cantilever arms and heavy support beams. Also arrived under tow from Singapore was the 300 ton sheerlegs barge *Sumpile 28*, which was to be our main salvage tool throughout the operation. Under the guidance of a specialist fabrication engineer, the six cantilevers together with their support beams were manufactured on shore, ready for later transportation to the salvage site. His job was not easy, using semi-skilled local labour on a bare stretch of mud under the blazing tropical sun.

On site, the salvage team were also hard at work. Four heavy Smit brackets were attached to the starboard side of the casualty and divers tunneled their way under the ship in order to run four 75 mm diameter wires to the river bank to hold the ship in position. These were connected via six-fold purchases to four 15 ton Danforth type anchors that had been buried ashore using bulldozers and an excavator.

Like all passenger ships, the *Leuser* had lots of openings such as sea intakes, overboard discharges, tank filling pipes, ventilation pipes, doors, windows, portholes and ventilators. Many hundreds of hours were spent prefabricating patches to fit each and every one of those openings. Where possible, the patches were fitted above the water on both sides of the vessel, but the rest were to be left to the team of divers after the ship had been righted.

Heavy 'I' beams and special brackets had first to be fitted to the hull to take the legs of the six metre high cantilevers. These were only fitted after all internal repairs had been completed and the main hull patch had been welded into position. In a two week period, hundreds of kilos of welding rods were used until all six cantilevers were finally placed in position and the starboard side of the ship was declared watertight. Ten fifteen ton anchors were then laid in a pattern across the river using the *Sumpile 28* and the tug *Sea Speed*. Shots of 75 mm diameter chain added weight to the anchor pattern, while heavy wires connected to the two pull barges, *Swissco Marine 9* and *Sea Warrior*. Forty ton hydraulic winches aboard the pull barges were each connected in turn to six-fold 200 ton safe working load tackles, each tackle being connected to one of the cantilevers.

The days were long; we worked from six in the morning until about eight at night, seven days a week. The salvage crew were housed on the *Swissco Marine 9*, with four berth cabins and a small recreation room. At least it was air conditioned which made for a good nights sleep, and we had plenty of fresh water for showers, but the tucker left a lot to be desired.

When all was ready to commence the uprighting operation, two large bulldozers were connected to the six-fold purchases ashore, between the restraining wires connected to the outboard of the *Leuser* and the four buried anchors. The *Sumpile 28* took up position at the bow of the casualty, and her 300 ton purchase blocks were connected to stabilise the ship once she became upright. Outboard of the vessel the two pull barges were positioned with six-fold purchases connected to the cantilevers and held fast by the anchor pattern laid across the river.

On the first attempt, winches and bulldozers combined to exert a pull of 1,500 tons to try to roll the vessel over. Slowly the vessel began to move and the 80-degree list was reduced to 35 degrees before she stopped and refused to move any further. The fact that the *Leuser* was a passenger vessel had caused the problem. Having so many decks and so many compartments, the free flow of air throughout the partially uprighted ship was restricted and his trapped air was now acting as buoyancy directly against the pulling and uprighting movement.

Operations were halted for two days while the divers released the trapped air by loosening off some of the patches and drilling holes through the hull. After the air had escaped, the ship was resealed and the uprighting operating recommenced. The *Leuser* was finally brought to rest with a list of 22 degrees to port. This was considered to be a safe angle; the salvors did not want her to flop over the other way. It was an angle that the salvors and diving crew could live with, as we continued to try and refloat the vessel via patching and pumping.

Although the bow of the ship was now above water, the stern was still well under. Patching operations continued, with the salvage crew working topsides and the diving teams patching underwater. The 22-degree list did not make the job easy, especially for the divers trying to manoeuvre the heavy steel patches below the overhang of the various decks. The main reason that the *Leuser* rolled over and sunk in the first place was due to flooding. With the engine room flooded through the collision damage, pipe work was broken allowing up flooding through the domestic plumbing system. Therefore we were very careful to plug every overboard discharge and sea intake prior to pumping. Extensive use was made of the Tornado underwater bolt gun for securing the patches in position. Finally, the vessel was completely sealed ready for pumping to commence.

Two large generators were landed aboard the casualty to provide light and power for the eight six-inch electric submersible salvage pumps, each capable of shifting 250 tons of water per hour. Three smaller electric submersibles, three air diaphragm pumps and two large diesel pumps were on standby for any eventuality. The Naval architect had calculated that some 17,000 tons of mud, water and debris had to be removed from inside the vessel. On the 59th day of the operation, pumping finally commenced. Two hours later nothing had happened, the inside water level remained constant and that night a great sense of disappointment prevailed.

Early the following morning, a rogue opening was found on the poop deck. It was a small ventilation grill, one that was not shown on the plans and that the divers had missed while working in the zero visibility. A patch was quickly manufactured and fitted and pumping recommenced. Within thirty minutes there was a noticeable fall in the level of the water inside the ship, and the pumps were lowered further down into the vessel.

The ship had been lying sunk for four and a half months and everything was covered in a thick layer of mud and slime. When we first arrived on site my pal Alan had said what a pity that the river was so dirty or else we could jump in to cool off. After working inside the ship for hours on end, the river looked relatively crystal clear. When we came off for a break we always headed for the overside ladder, hanging on for dear life in the strong current letting the river wash away the worst of the filth.

Working inside the casualty presented other difficulties. Moving about with the 22-degree list was extremely difficult and it was hard work lugging the 150 kg pumps and hoses down through the many decks and compartments.

During pumping the divers continued to check the outside of the ship. Many small openings were discovered and sealed as the pumping rate increased. Work continued day and night until day 63, when the ship finally lifted off the bottom with a seven-degree list to port and held in place with the 300 ton sheerlegs. After another three days she was practically pumped dry with only a one-degree list. The smaller electric pumps were then set up in the lower compartments and run intermittently to take care of the entrapped water from the upper decks as it found its way down to the bottom of the ship.

Meanwhile, a special team of men and equipment had been flown out from Germany and as soon as it was possible to access the engine rooms, machinery preservation was carried out on the main engines and generators. This was an important part of the salvage operation, as the ship was to be refitted for further trading and the salvors had to take all steps possible to minimise the loss for the owners and underwriters. As the ship had been lying for so long before salvage began, a large amount of mud had penetrated the vessel and this together with bedding, linen, carpets, rotting foodstuffs and over 1,200 waterlogged mattresses all had to be removed. All cabins and other spaces had to be hosed out and thoroughly cleaned: a major job in itself.

Once the ship was upright and stabilised, the six cantilever arms and their support beams had to be removed, involving a great amount of above and underwater cutting. Anchors and chains had to be recovered from the riverbed and from the pits ashore where they had dug deeply into the clay.

After all that work had been completed, the *Leuser* was then prepared for towage to a repair yard for refitting. Main and emergency towlines were rigged, lifeboats that had been landed ashore were reloaded aboard and many other jobs carried out to ensure that the ship arrived safely at her final destination. While lying ashore, although in full view of the salvage operation, the lifeboats had been completely stripped of diesel engines, shafts and propellers; just the bare hulls remained. We even lost a couple of our big shackles, huge 250 ton swl that took four men to lift. What was done with those in the local fishing village, I have no idea.

Water-tight doors were closed, propeller shafts locked, rudders secured and a three man running crew were placed aboard for the voyage, together with pumps, generators, air compressors and damage control equipment.

A surveyor from the Salvage Association inspected the vessel and a clean bill of health was issued on day 80 of the salvage operation. Under tow of the tug *Britoil 26*, the *Leuser* slowly made her way down river and headed on her ten day voyage to the repair yard. At long last a very difficult salvage job was completed. The whole operation was very similar to the *Herald of Free Enterprise* that had received massive publicity, when she sank in the North Sea in March 1987. The biggest difference being that Rainer Kasel and his crew had completed the job using only the minimum of equipment in a much more hostile environment.

At the repair yard the vessel was dry docked and repair work carried out. I can only assume that all our plugs in the hull were removed at that time. The vessel was taken out of the dry dock, placed alongside the repair berth and the shipyard stopped work for the day. The following morning, the poor old *Leuser* was back how we first found her, lying on her side sunk in the shipyard. Naturally we put in for the salvage job, knowing that it would be a lot easier to do the second time. However, the shipyard had a close association with a major salvage concern and they secured the contract. After many months she was finally raised again, refitted and is now sailing on her familiar routes through the Indonesian Archipelago.

On arrival back at Singapore, the boss flew Alan's wife and Roslyn up for a few days celebration and then it was back home to Eden after a very rewarding and exciting job.

Chapter 12

The Time the Locals Popped Round

The remainder of 1998 was fairly busy with survey work on the fishing fleet up and down the coast, but after Borneo it was rather uninteresting. One job that I was called to was a steel trawler aground on the entrance bar at Lakes Entrance. Unfortunately I was not advised until the whole disaster was over and I arrived on site in time to carry out a damage survey and start going through the salvage bills. I was horrified to say the least. The vessel had suffered a large amount of damage, the salvage effort was an expensive fiasco and the whole exercise cost the underwriters a lot of money. Through a number of phone calls and written reports, I strongly advised them to contact me as soon as an incident occurred, and that way they could perhaps save money.

In November another steel trawler went aground on the Lakes Entrance bar and that time I was advised immediately. Alan Cameron and myself took off for Lakes Entrance straight away. The trawler was near enough the same size as the previous one and had grounded within 50 metres of the earlier location. In a little over twenty-four hours of arriving on site, the vessel was refloated without damage.

Once again it was my job to add up all the bills including our charges. The cost to the underwriters for repair and salvage costs were roughly 10% of the previous case. Needless to say ever since that time, whenever a vessel gets into trouble on that particular bar, K Salvage is the first to be informed.

At the end of the year I picked up a delivery job on the dredger *Orwell*, a trailing split hopper from Karumba in Queensland to Honolulu. It was a pleasant run across the South Pacific, calling into Honiara on the way. After arrival I had a couple of days waiting for a flight home and managed to see a few of the sights in Honolulu, but I do not think that I shall be going back there for a holiday; the beaches in Eden are much better and far less crowded.

In early 1999 I was asked to prepare evidence for another court case. This was to do with the Antarctic Fishery, and took up a lot of time working from home before going down to the court in Melbourne. It was another interesting experience, but it was an area that I was not really familiar with so was glad when it had finished.

In May, Kasel Salvage obtained a contract to lift a cargo of containers off a small vessel stranded in Sulawesi, Indonesia, and I was called in to carry out the operation. From Singapore I flew with Jeff Watson and two salvage crew to Ujung Pandang in Sulawesi where we arrived about six o'clock at night. The local agent met us and we all piled into a mini-bus for another nightmare journey to the town of Palopo. The trip took nearly eight hours through jungle roads and I still shudder at the thought of how many times we nearly ran off the road, and how many times we should all have been killed in head-on collisions. Shaken and weary, we arrived at four in the morning. We found a local hotel, demolished half a bottle of my duty free rum and crashed out, exhausted.

The following day proved to be very frustrating, I was under a lot of pressure from Singapore to get out to the casualty, but we were in the back blocks of Indonesia and the words 'hurry' or 'move in haste' were completely unknown. The tug that had been hired in for the job was a beauty to say the least, and the entire day was spent filling her up with fuel, fresh water and stores as there was nothing aboard. I also managed to chase up some towing ropes, purchased four mattresses so we had something to sleep on, and got hold of some empty drums to transfer some fuel to the casualty.

The local agent in Palopo was quite a character. He owned the waterfront bar and was very hospitable. He told me that the tug captain had gone home (up country), so there was no need to rush things as we would not be sailing today anyway. As it turned out this probably worked in our favour, as the police, customs and harbour officials were all on hand, and after buying a few beers and handing out lots of cigarettes, everybody concerned could not have been more helpful.

At noon the following day, our missing captain appeared and we departed from Palopo on the good tug *Kimtrans Taurus*. Out in the roads we connected up to the large container barge *Kimtrans 88* and sailed south down Teluk Bone towards the casualty 140 miles away.

We laid our mattresses out on deck as there was no space inside, and tried to get a few hours sleep. At two in the morning we ran into a severe electrical storm and the heavens opened up with a tropical downpour that lasted all night. In a few minutes we were all soaking wet and the remainder of the trip was spent sitting wedged in a corner of the tiny mess room. The job had certainly gotten off to a good start. By seven the following morning I was aboard the casualty, while the divers conducted an underwater survey on the reef. She was nearly high and dry and the only way to discharge the container cargo was to work the tides and try to get the barge alongside at high water. The tug and barge were anchored off and I boarded the casualty using our onsite work boat, a dugout canoe with two out-riggers and a single cylinder diesel engine that would have felt at home in any museum.

The casualty was the *Armada Satya*, a 2,400 ton cargo ship that had seen better days. She had been aground for more than three months with the crew still living on board. They were buying food stores from the local villagers and catching rainwater, but had no fuel aboard for running the generators. With a lot of difficulty, fuel was transferred in drums from the tug via the dugout canoe until we could get the generator running and could use the derricks to start shifting hatches, beams and containers. The container barge was a good unit and the Chinaman operating the heavy lift-swinging derrick was even better. After three days, with the barge alongside for only a couple of hours each high water, all containers had been safely discharged.

The captain of the casualty was a nice bloke and I felt very sorry for him as there were no plans to refloat the vessel and they could be stuck out on that reef for months to come. I managed to contact Singapore and informed the boss that I could have her afloat within two days. The owners were contacted but refused to enter into a salvage contract and three and a half days after arriving on site, we set sail back to Palopo.

Before leaving I had a good yarn with the captain and transferred all the hatches and beams to the fore end of the ship to change her trim. I left him some written instructions and diagrams of what he had to do to refloat the vessel, including a list of which tanks to pump out and which to flood. She freed herself from the reef some time later, we were never going to get a salvage contract and as I said, I felt sorry for the bloke.

Our road journey back to Ujung Pandang that time was done in daylight and was a lot less nerve wracking. We arrived at a civilised hour in time for a nice hot shower and a decent meal. The following day it was back to Singapore to write up the report before the flight home.

In June I was contracted to fly up to Port Moresby and take over the tug *Pacific Salvor* (668 gross tons, built 1979) for Pacific Towing (PNG) Limited. The day before I was due to fly out, a desperate plea for help was received from a crowd whose construction barge had gone up on the rocks at Gabo Island, forty miles to the south of Eden. Acting in their best interests I arranged for a work boat to sail from Eden with pumps, generators, patching material and two men to assist them in whatever way possible. That whole exercise turned into a disaster, with the barge sunk, a large amount of my equipment lost with no recompense and the threat of civil action hanging over my head as they tried to lay blame for their own incompetence.

Whilst all this was going on, I was in Port Moresby trying to get the tug ready for sea. She was an ex-French vessel and was in a fairly poor state, but after a few days we managed to get most things working and sailed for Fremantle to pick up our tow. The run down to Western Australia was not too bad apart from a number of mechanical problems and the excessive rolling of the tug. Of all the tugs on which I had sailed, some larger but some a lot smaller, I have never known a ship to roll as much and as violently as the *Pacific Salvor*.

Our tow was the Howard Smith tug *Gurrong*, which had been built by Oceanfast in Western Australia but had not been completed prior to the yard going into liquidation. She was now heading across to Whangarei in New Zealand to be completed by Northport Engineering, before returning to work in the Port of Melbourne. We spent a week in Fremantle preparing the *Gurrong* for her 3500 mile tow. A great deal of equipment had to be loaded aboard and secured for sea passage, as well as securing the tug itself which when we arrived was minus watertight doors, hatches and numerous other fittings. Sea chests and pipe work had to be blanked off and an emergency bilge alarm fitted, which was connected to a strobe light on the mast of the tow.

After sailing, two days of good weather was experienced before heading across the Great Australian Bight. The run across the bight was something else, with continuous gale force winds and mountainous seas for the entire passage. Forty-foot seas and force ten winds for days on end took their toll; sleep was impossible and everything that could possibly break adrift did. Speed was reduced to nurse the tow and the towing gear, with our after deck constantly buried under six feet of water.

Thirteen days after leaving Fremantle we headed into Twofold Bay to check out the tow and take stock of damage. The connection at the tow end consisted of a single leg of two-inch diameter chain. When we arrived at Eden we discovered it was nearly worn through and it had to be replaced. If we had carried on, it is certain that the tow chain would have parted with possible disastrous consequences for the tow.

After two days anchored in Eden, we were on our way again in perfect weather and set off up the coast, prior to heading off across the Tasman Sea. The good weather again failed to last and before long we were in the midst of a SSE gale. The tug was rolling forty degrees either side in a roll period of six seconds; it was not a pleasant voyage. Eight days later we arrived in Whangarei and delivered our tow safe and sound and after a day repairing towing gear, proceeded back to Port Moresby. It had been rather a long ten weeks and I was happy to be on the plane back to Sydney. Although I was not over impressed with the tug I was more than happy with the local New Guinea crew who had turned out to be a really good bunch of fellows to sail with, and very willing to learn.

Once back at home I discovered all the hard work on the P & I course had seemingly paid off, for I was informed that my name was about to nominated on the list of Special Casualty Representatives under the new SCOPIC clause of the Lloyds Open Form of salvage agreement. That meant that I could be called in to attend a marine casualty as a special observer for the International Group of Protection and Indemnity Underwriters.

Being a long way from where all the action takes place and being an unknown quantity to the powers that be in London, I decided to head over to England and try to meet as many people as possible who were directly involved in the industry. I flew to London in October and for two weeks arranged a series of meetings with various representatives from the P & I Clubs and other organisations. It had been fifteen years since I'd last visited the UK, but it did not take me very long to find my way about. The Clubs that I visited made me very welcome and support was gained for my nomination to the SCR Panel. I just hoped that the expense of the trip would be justified in the long run with incoming work.

The year ended quietly and apart from a couple of possible jobs that never

Trawler Hewardia *at Marlo, Victoria*

eventuated from Rainer in Singapore, survey work kept ticking over until the next big one came along.

Early in the New Year a small steel trawler *Hewardia* grounded on an isolated stretch of coast near Marlo in Victoria and Alan Cameron and myself drove down at the request of the underwriters to see what we could do. With two four-wheel drive vehicles towing a trailer load of towing ropes and a bulldozer leading the way, we headed into the bush making our own tracks through the coastal swamps and sand hills in order to reach the casualty.

Two other fishing vessels were standing by offshore and two coils of heavy polypropylene towlines were floated out using messenger lines and an inflatable Zodiac boat. With a good dozer operator doing plenty of digging and pushing, the casualty was refloated within eight hours of us arriving on site. She was towed back to Lakes Entrance undamaged, while we packed up all the gear and headed home. Although only a small operation, the underwriters showed their appreciation most generously, for without expert guidance she could have well become a total loss given her isolated and exposed position.

Another job was in the pipeline for the Gippsland Ports Authority for a wreck removal contract. However, the decision took many months and yet again I had to rely on survey work, which was proving to be an important standby.

And so, after much deliberation, I took the decision to dispose of my salvage plant. A lot of money was tied up in the equipment, which after a number of years had not even come close to paying for itself. The rent on the industrial property was a constant drain on resources and the equipment maintenance was time-consuming and expensive. The ever-increasing rules and regulations did not make things any easier, added to that the high cost of worker's compensation and other regulatory requirements, including my hefty fine from Mr Workcover. Also, the episode at Gabo Island some time before had damaged an amount of machinery beyond repair, and I could not see the way clear to replace this equipment due to the huge expense involved.

I was lucky to find a willing buyer in my old mate Danny Dorman, who ran a diving business in Melbourne. In any future salvage jobs, I could use Danny's divers and hire back any of the equipment required, which seemed to be an excellent arrangement and saved me the trouble and expense of maintaining it. It was not long, however, before I was away again on another major salvage, which proved to be one of the most interesting. The job also opened up a whole raft of new contacts and managed to put me on a solid footing for future work.

Luck is the name of the game, including being on the right spot at the right time. My pal Captain Dave Hancox who was salvage master for United Salvage was overseas and I landed the job in his place.

The *World Discover* was an expedition cruise ship that travelled the world in search of adventure from the Arctic wastes to the Coral Sea. However on April 30th 2000, whilst cruising through the Solomon Islands, the ship struck a hidden reef in the Florida group of islands and rapidly began filling with water. Luckily, there were no serious injuries and all of the elderly passengers were evacuated into the lifeboats, being later taken to the Port of Honiara, while the captain ran the vessel ashore in a desperate bid to stop her from sinking in deep water.

At six the following morning the telephone rang. United Salvage had secured the salvage contract and my presence was required on site to act as salvage master. Out came my ever ready 'grab list', and my case was hurriedly packed according to the list, that way nothing is forgotten when you have to leave home at short notice for an extended period. Twenty-four hours later, on a chartered aircraft out of Brisbane with four salvage crew, we were circling the casualty. As we gazed out from high above, we could see that we did not have a very easy job ahead of us.

Men and equipment were mobilised from Australia, Papua New Guinea and Fiji. Less than a week after receiving the call, preliminary work had started on a long and difficult salvage operation. The ship was lying on her side with a list of 38 degrees, completely flooded throughout her length and at a very isolated location. The nearest town was the capital of Honiara, which at the time was suffering severe political unrest. We set up camp in the main resort hotel, but power failures and difficulties in communication added to our problems.

After an initial inspection of the casualty both above and below water, we returned to the hotel armed with plans and stability information. During the next couple of days a salvage plan was prepared together with a list of required salvage equipment, most of which would have to be shipped in from Australia. On day five, the tug *Pacific Salvor* (4,800 bhp, 668 gross tons) arrived in Honiara and after loading stores, bunkers and fresh water, I headed off towards Roderick Bay where the *World Discoverer* was stranded. Carefully manoeuvring between the reefs, both anchors were dropped and the stern of the tug was secured to the casualty in a Mediterranean moor. When up and running the salvage crew consisted of forty men, backed up by two tugs, a salvage barge and various small support vessels.

Large pits were dug in the foreshore and huge logs from a nearby timber camp were buried, to which heavy wires and ground tackle were attached to hold the ship in position and stop her from falling off the reef into deep water. Divers cut away damaged steelwork underwater and welded steel patches over the main holes, while some ninety heavy wooden patches were put in place over windows, doors and other openings in the hull, which were now underwater.

One could not have wished for a more picturesque location to carry out a salvage job, with white sandy beaches, beautiful coral reef and swaying palm trees. The ship had grounded outside the Roderick Bay Yacht Club, a palm thatched hut that welcomed a large number of cruising yachts, judging by the plaques that adorned the walls. The village chief, John, was a friendly enough fellow and arranged for local labour to assist us with the log pits and general 'pulley–hauley' work. We presented him with United Salvage boiler suit and official time book, which he religiously kept. Each Friday he would come aboard to collect the men's pay for the week. I luckily had a large stock of cigarettes, for every time I stepped ashore — ten times a day some days — I would always come back with an empty packet. The locals always had their hand out to cadge a smoke, but in return you received a wide grin and the pickaxe or machete seemed to swing just that little bit harder. They were a good crew, but trouble was brewing and was not long in coming.

Work proceeded well up until day 18 of the operation, when large numbers of canoes started to appear and several hundred locals were observed gathering on the beach. Chief John warned that people intended to loot and burn the vessel that night, but they were bad men from out of town, not like the people from his village who were all good men. Discretion being the better part of valour, plus the fact that it was no use arguing with 300 men armed with machetes, the tug and barge went out to a safe anchorage and observed the destruction and sounds of looting from a safe distance.

Roderick Bay Yacht Club

The following day some armed police arrived, the tug and barge shifted back alongside the casualty and salvage work continued. No fires had been started on board and none of the patching work had been disturbed, only mooring lines slashed and everything in the ship above water level had been smashed or looted.

It took a couple of days to repair the damage and rig new lines fore and aft to the trees to hold the ship in position once she came afloat. Ten large salvage pumps were placed aboard to begin a carefully planned sequence of de-watering the vessel. Strings of lighting were rigged and portable ventilation fans were set up to provide fresh air to the salvage crew working inside the vessel. Patching and pumping continued until the night of day 25, when heavily armed intruders raided the ship again. The police were out-gunned by our visitors so no resistance was put up to avoid the 'late night shopping'. Throughout that night the sounds of smashing glass and gunshots kept the salvage crew wide awake and also a little worried.

Two days later reinforcements arrived in the form of a heavily armed rapid response group from Honiara and the salvors could finally get on with the job. Fortunately, the salvage gear on board had once more not been touched and only a few of our wooden patches had been smashed to gain access to various compartments to make looting easier.

Oil spill booms were laid around the ship and pumping began in earnest only to stop again the following day — that time for a completely different reason. Rotting foodstuffs, decaying furniture, carpets and fittings plus rotting raw sewage had filled the lower compartments of the ship with deadly hydrogen sulphide gas. Further ventilation fans were rigged up and the salvage crew had to wear breathing apparatus inside the vessel. The air quality inside the ship was continuously monitored with gas detectors. Hydrogen sulphide is a very nasty gas; at first the 'rotten egg' smell is very noticeable, however after a short time all sense of smell is lost and men will start collapsing. Unless moved from the source immediately, death will quickly follow.

Our salvage engineers finally managed to rig up the ship's main ventilation fans. These were located on top of the accommodation and well clear of the water, power cables were run from the tug's switchboard and the pump crews could continue work inside the vessel with a greater degree of safety. However BA Sets were still used continuously with the recharging compressor going flat out to keep up the supply of air bottles.

Slowly, the vessel came further out of the water and the list was reduced to 30 degrees. The restraining tackles held her firmly in place, all the leaks had been sealed and the ship was finally afloat. Two more days of pumping were required before she would be ready to tow away. A heavy anchor and chain were laid offshore to hold the ship after she was finally pulled clear of the reef. Day 39 of the operation dawned, and the most pressing thought in the minds of the salvage crew was gaining access to D deck through further pumping. Located there was the ship's mortuary and on the good authority of the casualty's chief engineer, it was also stocked full of expensive French Champagne — just the thing to celebrate the end of a successful job.

Although we had helped ourselves to some liquid refreshments during the operation, the looters had taken most of the good stuff. It was heart breaking to see the damage done to the tastefully appointed accommodation, and most of the stolen articles would prove to be of no use to the looters. There was no electricity on the island and I am sure the locals would not be using the gyro compass repeaters or the three very expensive German sextants that went missing in their dugout canoes. Luckily, we had managed to save the ship's bell and this was presented to the grateful owner, where it is now possibly displayed on the new *World Discoverer*.

However we never did reach D deck and the champagne is still ageing, probably never to see the light of day again. The head of the rapid response group informed me that between 60 and 100 heavily armed militia were proceeding to the location from the eastern side of the island, intending to seize the ship and the salvage craft. He also said that they intended to take hostages and that he could no longer guarantee security. The situation was discussed with the director of United Salvage and the Special Casualty Representative. Satellite phone calls were made to London and the decision was made to abandon the vessel.

Once again, hordes of people started gathering on the shore. We continued work throughout the day to make everything appear normal; pumping continued, oil spill booms remained in place and our efforts were witnessed by more and more people gathering on the beach. Very discreetly, I took out one of our Zed Boats. The channel through the reefs was marked with buoys fitted with reflector tape that could be easily seen by torchlight.

As soon as darkness fell, the lighting on the casualty, barge and tug was extinguished and as much salvage gear as possible was recovered. A lot of gear was left behind unfortunately, but conditions were too dangerous and time was running out. The small tug and support craft slipped quietly away with all non-essential personnel and at nine o'clock I ordered the mooring ropes to be cut and the main tug with the salvage barge lashed alongside groped her way out through the reef-strewn entrance of Roderick Bay. The marker buoys laid earlier in the day guided us through the channel towards safety, as we were very much on our own.

That was a very disappointing end to a long and arduous job which was so close to being successfully completed. Ships and gear can be replaced, but the lives of salvage crew are far more precious. If only we'd had another forty-eight hours, the ship could have been towed to a safer anchorage and prepared for the sea tow to the repair yard. However, the *World Discoverer* lies stranded and forgotten in Roderick Bay, waiting to spill oil into the pristine wilderness and put to death by poison gas any who dare enter the abandoned hulk. Even today, two years after leaving the Solomons, the country is still in turmoil and I guess that the wreck will remain there until the next major cyclone pushes her off the reef into deeper water.

The vessel lies supported at either end by coral reefs with the tug and barge lying in a depth of approximately twenty metres. Ground tackles fore and aft hold the ship from slipping off the reef and into deep water, these are possibly still in place. Mooring lines can be seen fore and aft and the ship's lifeboats moored off the quarter.

The salvage contract was under a Lloyds Open Form incorporating the new scopic clause. Captain Nick Haslam had flown out from the UK to act as special casualty representative. As salvage master, I worked closely with Nick and hoped that the experience gained in the operation would prove beneficial, should I be called in to fulfil that role in any future scopic cases.

It was nice to get back home again and settle down after our close shave in the Solomons, but it was still a big let down, to be so near and yet so far from success.

Chapter 13

The Results of Networking

Another towing job came up in August so I flew to Thursday Island to pick up the small tug *Masthead* (159 gross tons) which had come down from Port Moresby to tow the log carrier *Ligaya* which had suffered engine failure in the Torres Strait. The *Ligaya* was a 7,000 ton deadweight cargo vessel fully loaded with timber and after taking bunkers and fresh water at Thursday Island, we went alongside the vessel anchored off Goods Island and connected the tow.

Unfortunately when the tug had been despatched from Port Moresby, she went to sea with only a single towline on board which was far too short and had no spare gear aboard whatsoever. The run up through the Great North East Channel went off fairly well, however once we left the inner route and the shelter of the reef, the short towline of only 200 metres caused problems.

We had a moderate following sea and swell and the speed of the tow had to be reduced in order to nurse our one and only towline. Very little sleep was had during the four day passage to Port Moresby, but finally the tow was safely delivered to the inner harbour and it was nice to get ashore for a decent sleep and a meal.

Hopefully my suggestions regarding towing gear have now been taken on board and the next time the *Masthead* puts to sea, she will be better equipped to handle the job. Once again the PNG boys proved themselves during the trip and they were a pleasure to sail with. With the tow safely delivered, it was back on the plane for home to await the next call.

The next job was different again, for instead of saving a ship, that time it was to go out to sea and sink one. (However, if I had been called in earlier, there may have been a chance of saving her.) I received a call from underwriters to go down to Lakes Entrance and interview the crew of a trawler that had been abandoned, on fire, in the Bass Straight. I met them as they were brought ashore in another fishing vessel. The report was not good: when they left the vessel she was well alight and slowly sinking.

Returning home, I contacted the New Zealand underwriters with my report. Things then came to a grinding halt as the decision on what to do with the wreck circulated between New Zealand, London and myself. It was not until *eleven* days after the vessel had been abandoned that I left Eden on the tug *Warringa* with a team of divers to locate the wreck, if still afloat. My instructions were to tow the vessel to deep water clear of the fishing grounds and sink her.

Our arrival on site the following morning presented flat calm weather conditions with only a slight swell. We were lucky with the weather as in any other sea conditions she would have been very hard to spot. The *Pacific Dynasty* was a modern trawler about 25 metres in length, but when we arrived all that was visible was about a metre of the stern protruding from the water. She was hanging vertically, barely afloat and tethered to the sea bed by her trawl wires, if we had been a day later she may not have been there at all.

The trawl wires were cut by explosive charges and the divers managed to secure the towing line to the rudder post. A gentle strain was taken and slowly the tug started to move her to deep water. After two hours the tow wire chafed through and once again the divers had to try to reconnect the gear. Ever so slowly she was moved away from the trawling grounds; if any more weight had been applied to the tow, she would have pulled under and gone straight to the bottom. Finally, deep water was reached just as the deck fittings tore away where the tow was connected and once again she was adrift.

Already air was escaping from the little buoyancy that remained and in order to sink her quickly, high-powered rifle fire blasted through her aluminium hull to speed her on the way. It was too dangerous for the divers to try to reconnect again and I did not want her drifting back towards the shallow water and fouling the fishing grounds. After a short time the vessel sunk in 800 fathoms and after collecting some floating debris, the tug sailed back to Eden. It is always a bit sad to see the death of a vessel, especially a smart modern trawler like the *Pacific Dynasty*. However, our job was done and we headed for home knowing that we had done our best.

Just days after arriving home, I received another telephone call, this time from Rainer Kasel in Singapore regarding a large bulk carrier that had caught fire and was immobilised off the north coast of Western Australia. Tsavliris, the Greek Salvor, had obtained a Lloyds Open Form of salvage agreement on the vessel and they required a salvage master to attend, prior to arrival of the salvage crew from Greece. Like a lot of overseas people, the principals failed to realise that Australia is rather a large place, and were disappointed when they were informed that I could not be on site within a few hours. As it was, within four hours of receiving the telephone call, I was on my way on the overnight bus to Melbourne, to catch a plane to Perth and Port Hedland, arriving there twenty-four hours after receiving their instructions.

The vessel was the Maltese bulk carrier *XL* of 80 624 gross tons. She had suffered an engine room fire (which they had extinguished) and she was anchored some fifty miles offshore. The following morning the local agent and myself proceeded to the casualty by chopper. For the next two days, arrangements were made to restore power to the vessel with portable alternator sets and to prepare the ship for onward towage to a repair port. There had been some loss of life associated with the fire and while aboard, I assisted the police with their investigation.

Two days later, the Greek salvage master and his team arrived on site and my job was over. Although the financial reward was hardly worth the effort involved, my policy has always been: never refuse an assignment. You never know when the big one will come up and in this game you don't get invited back a second time. Large salvage operations are definitely the most spectacular and gain a large amount of publicity. On the other hand, some small operations are just as difficult and can deliver just as much job satisfaction at the end of the day. The assignment that followed was one such case, the salvage, or more accurately the wreck clearance, of a small yacht.

Nearly twelve months had passed since I had driven down to Lakes Entrance to talk to the Port Authority regarding a ferro-cement yacht that had sunk in the entrance bar to the busy fishing port. I received another call and Danny Dorman and myself proceeded to Lakes Entrance to conduct a diving survey and discuss the operation. Within a day, the salvage contract was confirmed and we agreed to commence work the following week. A large amount of the salvage equipment that I had recently disposed of was put to good use and trucked to the port. The five-man salvage team consisted of Alan Cameron, Danny Dorman, two other divers and myself.

The vessel was the yacht *Ocean Reef* that had sunk on the entrance bar some sixteen months earlier. She was lying in the middle of the channel, completely buried and filled with sand. The entrance bar could change overnight depending on weather conditions and this was about the first opportunity where she was accessible. During the previous occasion when I had inspected the site with the Port Authorities, the channel had shifted to such a degree that it was almost possible to walk over the wreck without getting your feet wet. The wreck had to be shifted, as she interfered with dredging operations in the channel and the Port Authority could be held legally responsible if another vessel collided with the wreck and suffered damage.

To assist us in this operation we had the port's suction dredger *April Hamer*, used to dig trenches in the vicinity of the wreck. This allowed the sand that was 'air-lifted' by the divers to have somewhere to disperse to, instead of washing straight back again at the turn of the tide. Conditions were far from perfect with dive time limited to a short period either side of slack water, plus the fact that the work boat had to lay with seas breaking aboard when the waves peaked on the bar. Only daylight hours could be worked due to the exposed position of the wreck, breaking seas and strong tidal streams.

For eight days, work continued on sand removal, recovering debris and fairing off hull fittings that could puncture the air lifting bags during the refloating process. A mass of wires and chain had to be cut from the wreck and from a number of marker buoys that had been laid on site during the previous 16 months. All those preparations were very time consuming and two days were lost when weather prevented us from approaching the site.

Lifting strops were rigged around the hull and to various strong points, until on day nine of the operation we steamed out to the site ready to attach the lifting bags, even going as far as to close the port for the morning while the lifting took place. The previous night the wind had increased to a force five with a rough sea and moderate swell rolling over the wreck's location.

A diver was sent down to secure the mooring for the work boat, but was very soon back on board. Overnight, the wreck had become completely buried and we were back to square one. Airlifting began once again and throughout the day the top side of the hull was once again exposed, but the tides were becoming stronger and bottom time was becoming less and less.

The following day, the wreck was again buried from sight and we returned ashore to discuss the situation with the Port Authority. Trevor Rudge and myself proceeded out to the site but were unable to see anything due to the massive turbulence in the channel and suspended sand throughout the whole area. The tides had beaten us and it was decided to suspend operations until conditions improved. The gear was stored away and everyone went home feeling rather disappointed; one thing you can never beat is Mother Nature and it was useless trying to continue.

Ten days later we were back and work started all over again. The wreck had become buried again and after airlifting and attaching marker buoys, the dredger was called in once more to dig trenches in the vicinity. Since our last visit, she had suffered even more damage and hours were spent cutting away reinforcing rods that protruded from the broken hull. During the seven days that followed, we suffered the usual setbacks: sand build-up; strong points on the hull tearing away when lift was applied; damaged lifting bags. We all arrived at the overwhelming conclusion that concrete boats were a pox on mankind.

Finally all was ready, the airbags were blown to the surface and the wreck lay suspended underneath. The depth of water was too shallow for a clean lift and the wreck still dragged along the seabed as she was slowly towed inshore. Towing her along the channel and through the breakwaters, our biggest worry was that she would plunge to the bottom and block the port. The tides in the inner channel ran at five knots with little or no slack water between the ebb and the flood, so if she had gone down in that area we would have been there for months.

Fate must have thought otherwise and the Gods smiled on us that day. Ever so slowly, with a few heart-grabbing stops along the way, the wreck was finally brought to rest alongside the bank of the lake, ready for dragging ashore. A further day was spent in the outer channel, slinging and lifting the various bits and pieces that still remained, until all traces of danger had been removed from the fairway and the wreck had been safely landed.

It had been a highly rewarding job and back in the motel that night, celebrations continued well into the early hours of the morning. The following day the Port Authority closed down operations and all the port workers with the salvage crew were treated to a great barbecue, washed down with plenty of cold refreshments. The channel was clear, the danger of future litigation for the Port Authority had been removed and we all felt pleased with a job well done. Even though the job had involved a relatively small vessel, everybody involved gained from the experience and I know very well who will be called in, if ever such a situation arises again in the future.

In fact it wasn't long before I was called back to Lakes Entrance by the Port Authority; that time their dredger *April Hamer* was fast on the entrance bar. She was in no danger of sinking, but if left, could have been driven further ashore resulting in a major salvage operation and the closure of the port through silting. Once again luck was on my side and within a few hours of arriving aboard, she was pulled free. With alternate dredging on either side of the vessel, controlled manoeuvring of the main engines and the pull of two fishing vessels, she came free just before dark and was able to enter port under her own power. It could have been much worse but I was called in good time, the right action was taken early and the situation was not allowed to develop into something major.

The *Devprayag* was a somewhat larger vessel, an Indian bulk carrier of 47,350 deadweight tons. She had been waiting off the Port of Portland, Victoria at anchor, when she was driven ashore in heavy weather. United Salvage secured the Lloyds Open Form of salvage agreement and I was called in by the Protection and Indemnity Club to safeguard their interests in the case of an oil spill. The salvage tug *Keera* was despatched from Melbourne to attend the casualty and after some time awaiting suitable weather conditions, the ship was refloated with the line pull of the tug and discharge of ballast water.

David Hancox was Salvage Master for United and he conducted the refloating operation in his usual professional manner. We discussed options and jointly agreed on the best method of approach and all went smoothly. Anti-pollution measures were agreed with the Victorian Marine Board and as no pollution occurred, all involved were pleased with the outcome. Although that particular job was a straightforward and speedy operation, the positive results would hopefully lead to future work with the P & I Clubs.

Early in the morning of February 20th 2002, the telephone rang once more. After a number of false alarms since my previous assignment, an immediate start was required and within one hour of taking the call I was boarding the plane at Merimbula airport. The Panamanian ship *Jody F Millennium* had been driven ashore at the Port of Gisborne on the east coast of New Zealand's north island. A crew from United Salvage was already on site. However, the salvage master David Hancox requested my services as assistant salvage master, and the following morning I boarded the casualty from the Gisborne pilot boat.

The casualty was loaded with 20,000 tons of logs including a full deck cargo, some of which had already been washed over the side in the severe weather conditions. Her bunkers contained over 640 tons of heavy fuel oil plus diesel fuel and already some pollution had occurred through ruptured double bottom tanks. The grounding had taken place on one of New Zealand's favourite surfing beaches, creating much public concern.

Before my arrival on site, weather conditions could not have been worse, with a heavy sea and swell driving the vessel directly onto the shoreline. Captain Hancox had managed to ballast the ship down to try and prevent further movement, and the majority of the heavy fuel in the double bottom tanks had been transferred to the high wing ballast tanks to prevent any more pollution. A small amount of the heavy fuel had been transferred ashore, but conditions on site made this operation both difficult and dangerous. Finally, the local authorities were convinced that the fuel transferred to the wing tanks was better off left where it was, and arrangements were put in hand to discharge some cargo prior to refloating.

The tug *Keera* (470 grt, 4,800 hp) had been despatched from Melbourne and the *Pacific Chieftain* (1297 grt, 6,000 hp) sourced from her oil field work in New Zealand. With both vessels connected to the casualty and ground tackle laid out to hold her in position, cargo discharge commenced. Luckily, the vessel was fitted with very good deck cranes, and while these discharged cargo over the side into one of the large sea tow barges, helicopters were used to great effect transferring the cargo directly ashore. In the meantime ballast water was pumped out and the damaged tanks pressurised with air to gain further buoyancy.

At one stage, up to three helicopters were working on the discharge lifting 1–2 ton loads and dumping them at a pre-arranged log dump on the foreshore. The turnaround time was very quick and what was more surprising, given the tonnage handled that way, was that the use of helicopters proved to be quite cost effective. I must add that those choppers spent most of their time working in the timber industry; therefore the crews involved knew exactly what they were doing.

On the afternoon of February 24th, the casualty was pulled free of her stranded position and towed to a safe anchorage. All compartments were closely monitored to check for any ingress of water and the vessel prepared for towage to the port of Tauranga. It was intended that at Tauranga, all remaining cargo would be discharged. More permanent repairs would also be carried out to allow an onward towage to a final repair port, which was at this stage still undecided.

We departed Gisborne on the evening of Wednesday 27th under tow of the *Keera*, berthing at Tauranga three days later. Luckily the weather was good for the passage, as the tow was made more difficult by the fact that the rudder of the casualty was jammed hard over to starboard. For the two weeks that followed, work continued alongside the wharf at Tauranga. All cargo was discharged and repair work on the hull of the vessel was put in hand. The sheltered waters of the harbour made working conditions very good for the divers, although the strength of the tidal streams limited the hours of work underwater.

Jody F Millennium *ashore at Gisborne, New Zealand*
(courtesy of Gisborne Herald, New Zealand)

The jammed rudder, the stock of which was badly distorted, was removed together with the skeg; both landed back aboard. Large and small steel patches were manufactured and secured by divers to make the hull watertight, with smaller cracks secured by soft wood wedges and epoxy. The final phase of the patching operation was to construct a large cement box underneath number five hold in the damaged double bottom tank with some fifty tons of cement poured in position.

Portable pumps and damage control gear were placed aboard and the main and emergency towing gear were rigged for her final passage. The Lloyds Salvage Form was terminated on March 16th and the *Jody F Millennium* departed under tow of *Keera* some days later.

That was the end of another interesting job and, as in every case, the learning process continued. The job attracted a lot of media attention and at the end of the day, all parties were more than happy with the final result. In other words the work of the salvors were appreciated, a rare event in this day and age.

Just a couple of weeks after arriving home, I received an urgent call to proceed down to Lakes Entrance as another trawler was up on the beach. Within the hour Alan Cameron and myself once again headed south to find the small steel trawler *San Rafael* washed up on the beach some distance east of the entrance. That evening we managed to make an inspection of the vessel, but the light and the tides were both falling so we returned to town and made plans for the following day's high tide.

Access was again our biggest problem and several hours were spent mobilising equipment over sand dunes and along the beach to the location of the casualty. Towlines were run offshore to two towing vessels, while a bulldozer dug a trench alongside the vessel, enabling the rising tide to do most of the hard work in setting her free. Just about on top of the tide while using the bulldozer to push, disaster struck. The dozer blade punched a neat hole right through the hull and for a short time I thought that we had lost her. Hurriedly, soft wood wedges were hammered into the hole and panel beater's 'bog' slapped on to make an almost watertight seal. The vessel came free, was safely towed into port and secured alongside. The timing was perfect as we could still make the pub before last orders.

Things quietened down for a while after that, and I procured one standby role after another with no real job ever eventuating. I worried that I was reaching the end of the story, even though I was nowhere near ready for that dreary world of retirement. Living in the sleepy hollow of beautiful Eden, some 12,000 miles away from London, the old adage "out of sight, out of mind" couldn't have been truer.

Finally, the telephone rang in September 2002, and I was on my way to the north coast of Western Australia to attend the loaded bulk carrier *Hanjin Dampier*

(205,000 ton) aground off the Port of Dampier. That was followed by the 56,000 ton car carrier *Hual Europe* in October that had been blown ashore on the coast of Oshima Island south of Tokyo. At four o'clock in the morning, just two weeks before Christmas, the phone on the bedside table rang once again. Hours later and I was in the air, heading towards Sydney on a small charter plane to attend the 46,000 ton bulk carrier *Western Viking*, aground off the coast of Qatar in the Persian Gulf.

2003 got off to a slow start. However in March I took a short drive up the coast to attend the fishing vessel *Bianca B*, which had grounded on a rocky ledge tearing the fibreglass hull completely open. With no prospect of any financial return for underwriters, she was dismantled in place after receiving a wreck removal order from local authorities.

In May I was standing on the airstrip at Merimbula once more, awaiting sunrise and enough light for the chartered Cessna aircraft to depart for Sydney. That would be followed by a connecting flight to Fiji and the Taiwan fishing vessel *Fong Kuo No. 6*, heavily aground on an isolated reef some sixty miles to the east of Suva. Once again I was back working with my old friends from United Salvage who had secured the contract. That time, however, my job was to oversee the operation on behalf of the underwriters, as the salvage master was Eric Johnson who had flown out from the UK arm of the company. Although only a relatively small vessel of 56 metres in length, her isolated and exposed position did not make for a simple operation. Eric and his team put in many long hours before the vessel was safely redelivered to her owners in Suva.

My next assignment was the chemical tanker *Al Farabi* in Taiwan as salvage expert for her owners. She had grounded off the southern port city of Koahsiung during typhoon Imbudo, and although relatively undamaged was heavily ashore and rapidly settling into the seabed. By careful ballasting down, the vessel was secured before two relief tankers lifted over 10,000 tons of cargo in a ship-to-ship transfer operation. She was then successfully refloated by Asian Salvage Company tugs.

That was a rather unusual assignment. Although a Lloyds Form of Salvage Agreement had been signed with a local company, it was up to me to call the shots, as the company involved had limited salvage expertise. However, all worked out well in the end through good co-operation of all parties involved.

While all these things were taking place, I received a telephone call from the leading firm of Australian Underwriters requesting my assistance. This was to prepare counter-evidence in a large salvage operation with which they had been involved in. That was a new contact for me and following a successful outcome, I hoped that they would make use of my services again at some time in the future.

2004 brought a variety of work, such as a loaded coal carrier aground in Taiwan, another trawler aground at Lakes Entrance, a container ship ashore in Mid Pacific and two more assignments for the London lawyers. Those jobs all came from different sources, and it appeared that all my hard work had finally started to reap rewards.

If those twelve months are anything to go by, I can look forward to a few more busy years before its time to hang up the overalls and take up lawn bowls.